The World's Best

CATFISH COOKBOOK

by Stan Warren

Stoeger Publishing Company, Accokeek, Maryland

STOEGER PUBLISHING COMPANY
is a division of Benelli U.S.A.

BENELLI U.S.A.
Vice President and General Manager:
  Stephen Otway
Director of Brand Marketing and
  Communications: Stephen McKelvain

STOEGER PUBLISHING COMPANY
President: Jeffrey Reh
Publisher: Jay Langston
Managing Editor: Harris J. Andrews
Design & Production Director:
  Cynthia T. Richardson
Photography Director: Alex Bowers
Imaging Specialist: William Graves
Sales Manager Assistant: Julie Brownlee
Editorial Assistant: Christine Lawton
Administrative Assistant:
  Shannon McWilliams
Proofreader: Celia Beattie

Published by Stoeger Publishing Company
17603 Indian Head Highway, Suite 200
Accokeek, Maryland 20607

BK0325
ISBN: 0-88317-270-4
Library of Congress Control Number:
2002115930

Manufactured in
the United States of America.

Distributed to the book trade and
to the sporting goods trade by:
Stoeger Industries
17603 Indian Head Highway, Suite 200
Accokeek, Maryland 20607
301-283-6300 Fax: 301-283-6986
www.stoegerindustries.com

OTHER PUBLICATIONS:
Shooter's Bible 2004 - 95th Edition
  The World's Standard Firearms Reference Book
Gun Trader's Guide - 26th Edition
  Complete Fully Illustrated Guide to Modern
  Firearms with Current Market Values
Elk Hunter's Bible
Shotgunning for Deer
Trailing the Hunter's Moon
Hunt Club Management Guide
The Turkey Hunter's Tool Kit: Shooting Savvy
Hunting Whitetails East & West
Archer's Bible
The Truth About Spring Turkey Hunting
  According to "Cuz"
The Whole Truth About Spring Turkey
  Hunting According to "Cuz"
Complete Book of Whitetail Hunting
Hunting and Shooting with the Modern Bow
The Ultimate in Rifle Accuracy
Advanced Black Powder Hunting
Hounds of the World
Labrador Retrievers
Hunting America's Wild Turkey
Taxidermy Guide
Cowboy Action Shooting
Great Shooters of the World
Sporting Collectibles
The Working Folding Knife
The Lore of Spices
Antique Guns
P-38 Automatic Pistol
The Walther Handgun Story
America's Great Gunmakers
Firearms Disassembly with Exploded Views
Rifle Guide
Gunsmithing at Home
Complete Guide to Modern Rifles
Complete Guide to Classic Rifles
FN Browning Armorer to the World
Modern Beretta Firearms
How to Buy & Sell Used Guns
Heckler & Koch: Armorers of the Free World
Spanish Handguns
The Handloader's Manual of
  Cartridge Conversions
Modern Sporting Rifle Cartridges
Complete Reloading Guide
Ultimate Bass Boats
Bassing Bible
The Flytier's Companion
Deceiving Trout
The Complete Book of Trout Fishing
The Complete Book of Flyfishing
Peter Dean's Guide to Fly-Tying
The Flytier's Manual
Flytier's Master Class
Handbook of Fly Tying
The Fly Fisherman's Entomological
  Pattern Book
The Legend of Harley-Davidson
The Legend of the Indian
Best of Harley-Davidson
Classic Bikes
Great Trucks
4X4 Vehicles
Fish & Shellfish Care & Cookery
Game Cookbook
Dress 'Em Out
Wild About Venison
Wild About Game Birds
Wild About Freshwater Fish
Wild About Waterfowl

* Special thanks to Keith Sutton–catfisherman extraordinaire–
for additional catfish stories, photographs and information.

Credits: pp.4, 5, 11, 51, 73, 108;
Duane Raver/USFWS

Contents

Catfish

"There is a species of fish that never looks at the clothes of the man who throws in the bait, a fish that takes whatever is thrown to it, and when once hold of the hook never tries to shake a friend, but submits to the inevitable, crosses its legs and says, 'Now I lay me,' and comes out on the bank and seems to enjoy being taken. It is a fish that is a friend of the poor, and one that will sacrifice itself in the interest of humanity. …We allude to the bullhead."

—George W. Peck, 1923

Introduction

If you have dropped a baited hook into a body of water in the United States, a catfish no doubt got at least a distant whiff of its aroma. From well inside the Canadian border to south of the Rio Grande, whiskerfish are an important part of the native fish population of most lakes, rivers, streams and even ponds so small that you wonder they can support fish at all. A quick look at the major players to be found in North America is in order.

CHANNEL CATFISH

From the small, skillet-sized "fiddlers" on up through heavyweight proportions, the channel catfish is arguably one of the most important. I have caught members of the tribe while fishing for walleye and yellow perch in Quebec and Ontario, and my heaviest to date came from the Salt River in Arizona. My first was caught below Pickwick Dam in Tennessee almost 40 years ago, so the channel and I are old acquaintances.

As catfish go, this is a rather handsome specimen. The upper portion of the body varies somewhat and will range from bluish gray to olive in color. There will be some speckles on the body, but the darkness and number of the spots differ from one area to another. At spawning time, males may turn virtually blue-black but will return to lighter hues after they spawn.

This is the fork-tailed fellow with a reputation for striking artificial lures. They will indeed do just that, and I have had a couple of bass fishing buddies surprised in the past. What they initially figured to be a bragging-sized largemouth turned out to be a healthy whiskerfish.

BLUE CATFISH

The blue is generally considered to be the giant of North American catfish, and with recorded

BLUE CATFISH

weights in the 120-pound class that title seems deserved. The majority may run 2 to 15 pounds, but oversized specimens show up often enough to allow an angler to realistically hope for that one big strike.

This is another fork-tailed catfish, and it prefers the clean, moving water that characterizes many legendary fishing holes such as those along the Tennessee River system. Being versatile, it can also do quite well in ponds and therefore is commonly "farmed" for the market as well as being stocked in farm ponds and small lakes.

Just for the record, the so-called "white catfish" caught in this neck of the woods is actually nothing more than a color phase of the blue. The bona fide white cat seldom exceeds 3 pounds.

FLATHEAD CATFISH

I must admit to a personal fondness for this fish despite its smooth, often oddly mottled skin and tiny, wide-set eyes. More than once my jig or spinner has come to an abrupt halt when a flathead (appaloosa cat, willow cat, or whatever) decided that it looked edible. Like the channel catfish, flatheads will occasionally grab artificial lures.

Another point in the flathead's favor as far as I am cocerned is his diet. Forget smelly concoctions and chunks of overripe shad, chicken entrails or meat scraps; the gent with the strangely shaped head likes his meals on the hoof and alive. Since this means that he will, under the cover of darkness, prowl the shallows in search of prey, he is the one who often inhales bluegill, shiners and other baitfish used on trotlines and limb lines.

THE BULLHEADS

Although they lack the commercial and sporting importance of the larger catfish, it is impossible to completely ignore the lowly bullheads. For many of us who grew up fishing in small creeks and farm ponds, these slick and finny critters were the first catfish that we even encountered on a person to fish basis. There is no need to go into detail concerning the brown, black, yellow and flat bullhead. Suffice to say that anything over a pound is unusual, 2 pounds is a whopper, and if they stick a fin into you it is going to hurt. The best way to get even for being stabbed is by eating the perpetrator. Bullheads are quite tasty despite being tedious to clean.

Care & Cleaning

With any fish, proper care while on the water will improve the culinary aspects.
Depending upon the actual type of fish, water and air temperatures, most usually
survive quite nicely in a livewell or on a stringer unless you overcrowd them.
To realize fish at their best, however, a large cooler is the way to go.

I prefer a cooler of at least 48-quart capacity, and for extended outings or when the need to keep a big specimen might arise then a 60- to 100-quart cooler is better. Naturally there needs to be ice in the thing, but long ago I found that a mix of half water and half ice works best. The fish chill quickly, plus they can't lie on top of the ice and play racquetball against the lid with their tail. I once had a 30-pound blue catfish literally launch the top off a name-brand cooler. The plastic missile narrowly missed my head as I buzzed across Kentucky Lake at about 50 miles an hour.

The ice water will not kill the fish, but does make them considerably more docile when cleaning time rolls around. It also ensures that the whole fish, fillets or steaks will be firm and tasty when the cooking begins.

Cleaning a fish is as simple or as complicated as you make it. On most occasions I fillet my catch although some types and a few recipes call for scaling or skinning. Most of you are probably proficient enough to handle this chore without any advice from the author, but I cannot resist passing along some pointers on handling catfish.

To clean a catfish, the basic procedure runs like this: make a cut behind the gills from the backbone to the belly on each side, then a slit down the back along both sides of the backbone and around the dorsal fin. The back cut is not strictly necessary, but does make skinning easier. Using pliers, pull the skin off each side, alternating as you go to prevent tearing the meat.

With a small fish, say from 3 pounds downward, this is a simple matter. For larger ones, some method of holding them is an asset. In days gone by, we simply nailed them to a handy tree or the side of the barn. My grandfather's barn and a large part of his apple orchard occasionally smelled pretty ripe during the summer months of years gone by. Nails, some sort of clamp, or even a sturdy eyehook are all helpful, and regardless of the setup used, give the fish a hefty thump between the eyes with something substantial. This will keep his flopping to a minimum.

When removing the entrails of a freshly skinned catfish, as well as most other species, trim away the belly flaps right up to the bottom of the ribs. This is not much of a waste since it is made up more of fatty tissue than tasty meat. It is also one of the places where unwelcome chemicals collect in waters that are anything but pristine.

Also, make sure that you remove the air sac or bladder near the top of the body cavity. Above it, right along the spine, you will see a dark "blood streak" which is actually the fish's kidney apparatus. With your thumbnail, a brush, or other implement, scrape it clear if the fish are to be fried whole or as steaks. The taste of your catch will be improved.

After skinning, some fish will be ready for the skillet just like they are. Anything over a pound that is slated for frying whole will benefit from being scored; that is, having cuts made down the sides 2 to 3 inches apart. This allows them to rinse more completely and fry more evenly. Larger ones will need to be cut into steaks, but for anything over a couple of pounds my choice is to convert them into fillets.

If you are used to filleting scaled fish, especially easy ones like sauger, bass or walleye, catfish can pose a few problems. One is in the form of a bony projection on the upper, front portion of the body. Being simplistic at heart, I simply begin my filleting cut behind that projection with my

electric knife, then use a regular blade to remove the chunk of meat forward of the trouble spot.

Whatever method you use, rinse the fish after cleaning in cold water and get them back under refrigeration. If they are not going to be eaten soon, freeze them rather than allowing them to sit around losing flavor. Catfish and most other species are best if eaten within 6 months. Back when milk came in waxed cardboard boxes, the perfect freezer receptacle was available for free. Now, freezer boxes or bags are fine, but fill each container with water to avoid freezer burn.

If your cooking plans call for using the fish in a day or so, small fish will keep nicely in nothing more than cold water. I normally add a tablespoon or so of salt, but that may be more out of habit than necessity. For large fish, whole, filleted or in steak form, you might want to add both salt and the juice from a lemon to the water. This is especially true if the water they came from was not pure and sweet, or if the larger fish might have a stronger taste than you prefer. People have different tastes. One friend of mine prefers steaks off the biggest catfish that he can find while his nephew, another fishing buddy, declares that only the little "fiddlers" of a pound or so are fit to eat without deodorizing.

Cooking Basics

When I was a lad, the only way that any fish was cooked was simple: fried. Cholesterol had not been invented, so my mother, grandmother, and various aunts who fed me on occasion simply scooped up a large glob of lard which we had rendered from our own hogs and plunked it down in a big, black, cast iron skillet to heat. The fish, usually whole ones, were dredged in cornmeal to which some salt and pepper had been added. Once the melted hog fat reached the right temperature, more or less, the frying began.

When my cousins and I made camping trips to the "Deep Woods," usually within a couple of hundred yards from one of our houses, fish cooked with lard in an old iron skillet over an open fire was always on our menu. That sounded great on the school bus or while working in one of the fields, but the naked truth was something else.

We envisioned a repast like those shown in sporting magazines of the day, beautifully browned fish properly enhanced by a few traces of hickory smoke, ready to be eaten by the light of a glimmering campfire. As we reached our teens, we finally decided that girls were more fun than camping, and we certainly figured out that there were easier ways to cook fish. There was also no need to keep a wet burlap bag on hand to extinguish either a flaming skillet or smoldering cook. Our parents and teachers were glad when the change came, too. They had thought for several years that an unknown illness had left us with permanently reddened eyes.

With the current emphasis on eating right and following the guidelines of culinary correctness, it is slightly puzzling to me to think that three of my grandparents lived to be well over 90 years of age. One grandmother only made it to 86, but she was a diabetic. Maybe they just did not know that foods fried in lard were not good for them. They certainly never worried about it.

In more recent times, I have fried small fish in bacon drippings left from breakfast. These were on back-country trips when packing too much gear is a problem such as when canoeing down waterways like the remote Big South Fork of the Cumberland River in north-central Tennessee. Most of the time I am a solid believer in cooking oil. Canola oil is a longtime favorite and does a fine job. I especially prefer it for frying trout. Peanut oil is favored by many, but it has been known to upset tender stomachs.

Oils are available today that are low in cholesterol and saturated fats, so by all means stick with them. Rather than insisting on a particular type, my preference is to carefully regulate the heat, keeping it at no less than 320 degrees and no more than 360 degrees while frying; 340 is perfect. Unless you scorch them by cooking at too high a heat, or turn excess breading material into a smelly, black residue, oils can be used several times with no problems. After each cooking session, allow the oil to cool and drain it through an old piece of cloth, or even better, a coffee filter, and it will remain quite serviceable. If it starts to take on a fishy aroma or any smell other than that of the basic oil, dump it and start over.

As an aside let me add that one of the best Cajun cooks that I know begins each session by heating the grease, then dropping a large peeled and quartered potato into it prior to starting the fish. She says that the spud "freshens" the grease. I have never found a reason to argue with her, largely because she is one heck of a cook. She also outweighs me by 100 pounds or so.

BREADING MATERIALS

While the traditional breading material for fried fish begins, and usually ends, with cornmeal, there are other options available. Even cornmeal offers some variety. Either plain or self-rising will work nicely, but I normally stick with the latter since it allows me to get into the hush-puppy batter mode without making any changes.

Yellow cornmeal tends to have a somewhat sweeter taste than the white variety, so let your taste be your guide. Since yellow tends to be a bit more coarsely ground, a case can be made for cutting it with flour if you like.

For skillet-sized fish, experiment a bit. Seasoned flour—flour with salt, pepper, and a dash of onion powder—works wonderfully on small fish. The delicate texture of the meat complements the lighter breading and is not covered up by the taste of the crust.

Another breading material that is used all too seldom is nothing more than crushed crackers. I'll cover this in more detail later in this book.

UTENSILS

Cooking utensil assortments can begin simple, but devout cooks will find them growing as time passes. For now you will need a fair-sized cast iron skillet with lid, a long fork, tongs, sharp knife, and a couple of medium-sized saucepans. Have a mixing bowl or two on hand as well. My current arsenal has enough Lodge brand cast iron skillets, Dutch ovens and other hardware to handle the feeding of an infantry battalion, but it is all used because of the different cooking needs that arise. Never, ever skimp on your basic cooking tools: use cast iron or a good, heavy-gauge commercial stainless steel unit.

PAN FRYING

This is fish cookery reduced to basics, at least in the beginning. A skillet, some oil, and seasoning and you can put a tasty meal on your plate, using any kind of heat source. Tinker with it if you will but be prepared to shell out a few extra dollars as you go along. Cheap equipment is more expensive in the long run, which is why most of us old-timers have cast iron skillets and deep-frying cookers that are deeper than they need to be. Cast iron transfers heat wonderfully well as do some of the copper-bottomed pots and even very thick aluminum.

Deep cookers mean that you can use a larger volume of oil, which allows better heat control, plus they don't let things get crowded when you have a horde of hungry mouths hanging around waiting for those fillets, French fries, hush puppies and such. Start big—you can downsize later.

Pan Frying Tips

1. Hurrying is a mistake when frying fish. If you don't have a cooking thermometer that tells you that the heat has reached 320+ degrees, use a pinch of bread or even breading material. When dropped into the oil they should immediately sizzle and dance, but at no time in the early stages of cooking should there be any smoke, which indicates that things are getting too hot. Too little heat and you will have greasy fish. Too much heat and you will burn the outside while the inner portions, especially on whole fish, may not cook completely.

2. After your cooking is done and your guests are round-bellied and happy, sneak away long enough to start your cleanup process. Let your cooker or skillet cool; then wipe out thoroughly with paper towels or soft cloths. For cast iron, this is all that you need to do unless you goof and really burn something. Deep fryer pots can be washed with detergent. If the oil hasn't burned, cool and drain. I use an old coffee maker with the heating element removed for the final step.

Hush-Puppies

"I do not know where, among the cornbreads, to place
hush-puppies. There are elevated Floridians who turn
up their noses at hush-puppies, but any huntsman
would not exchange a plate of them for crêpes
suzettes. They are made and served only in camp, or
when one is frying fresh-caught fish informally at
home, with the returned fishermen clustered comfort-
ably in the kitchen while the cook works. Hush-puppies
have a background, which is more than many fancy
breads can claim. Back of them is the hunt, the fishing
trip, the camaraderie, the grease in the Dutch oven
aromatic to hungry sportsmen. First you fry your
pristine fish, boned and filleted, rolled in fine cornmeal and salt and dropped into sizzling fat. You lift
out the fish, gold-brown, and lay them on pie plates
close to the camp fire. While they have been frying,
you have stirred up a mixture: fine white cornmeal,
salt, a little soda or baking powder, an egg or two or
three if the camp be affluent, and, if you want hush-
puppies de resistance, finely chopped raw onion. You
make the mixture dry and firm. You pat it into little
cakes or croquettes between your hands and drop the
patties into the smoking deep fat in which the fish have
been fried. They brown quickly to the color of winter

continued on page 14

Basic Pan-Fried Fish

Wherever fish are found on the menu, this recipe or some minor variation of it will be in use. It can be used with fillets, steaks, or whole fish, preferably those of under 2 pounds.

1. Preheat about 1 inch of oil in the skillet to 330 to 350 degrees.

2. Sprinkle fish with salt and pepper, then dredge in corn meal, or put all 3 ingredients into a bag, add the fish and shake well to thoroughly coat it. Carefully place fish in the heated oil.

3. When the fish has become lightly browned on the lower side, turn it over with tongs. Do not be in a hurry or undercooked breading will crumble away.

4. Repeat this until the fish is a uniform, medium brown. Cooking time will vary depending on the size of your catch. Small ones may be ready in 4 to 5 minutes with larger ones taking proportionally longer.

5. When the flesh flakes easily, remove the fish from the oil and drain it on paper towels.

Materials needed:

Large skillet (cast iron, of course)
Long fork or tongs
Cooking oil
Cornmeal
Salt & pepper

Undercooked fish should not be eaten, and overcooked ones are tough and have lost their flavor.

This is the traditional dish to be served with French fries, coleslaw and hush puppies with a big slice of white onion on the side. Ketchup is the condiment of choice here for both dredging potatoes and dipping fish. Iced tea or a cold beer will serve admirably to wash it down.

* Since you already have the ketchup out, mix some in a 4-2-1 ratio with grated horseradish and lemon juice. A dash of Tabasco won't hurt the mixture, either.

oak leaves, and you must be sure to have your coffee and any other trifles ready, for when the hush-puppies are brown, your meal is ready.

They must be eaten so hot that they burn the fingers that lift them, for the licking of fingers, as with the Chinese genius who discovered roast pig, is the very best of it. Do they sound impossible? I assure you that under the open sky they are so succulent that you do not care whether you have the rest of your dinner or not."

A Treasury of Southern Folklore
—Benjamin A. Botkin, 1949

Stan's Hush Puppies

1. Pre-heat oil to 325 degrees

2. Combine meal, onion, jalapeño and spices with enough milk (3/4 to 1 cup) to make a thick batter.

3. Use a teaspoon to dip a rounded portion of batter and place it in the hot oil. Rinse the spoon in clean water before each use so that the batter slides off easily.

4. The hush puppies will turn golden brown and float when done.

Materials needed:
2 cups cornmeal
1 egg
1/2 cup onions, chopped
1/4 cup jalapeño
   peppers, chopped
   (optional)
1 tablespoon black
   pepper
A pinch of sage

Deep-Fried Catfish

This is a variation of the previous recipe. While it can be done in the kitchen, many people prefer to do it outside and even make a social event of it. Commercial gas-fueled cookers are available, or a propane camp stove can serve as the heat source.

1. Preheat oil to 330 to 350 degrees. Use a thermometer rather than guessing.

2. Sprinkle fish with salt and pepper, then dredge in corn meal, or put all 3 ingredients into a bag, add the fish and shake well to thoroughly coat it. Carefully place fish in the heated oil.

3. When cooking several fish, add them gradually so that the temperature of the grease does not drop excessively. This will lead to mushy, oily results.

4. When the fish floats to the top and has a rich brown color, remove it from the oil and drain on paper towels. The flesh should flake easily.

Materials needed:

Large pot or Dutch oven
  (4- to 6- quart capacity
  minimum)
Tongs or slotted spoon
Oil to fill half of pot
Cornmeal
Salt & pepper
Onion salt (optional)

Also, tell the bystanders who are looking over your shoulder and licking their chops to let the object of their attention cool a moment. Being in a hurry can sizzle a lip.

* French fries, hush puppies, slaw, onion slices are standard side dishes, but try freshly cooked pinto beans.

Jugging for Catfish

"Very interesting sport in fishing for the channel cat is indulged on the Upper Missouri River, by both ladies and gentlemen. The following is the modus operandi: A party with several scull boats rendezvous above a rapid in the river, and to the handles of several dozens of empty jugs, well corked, they attach to each a line about four feet in length, rigged with a strong hook, well baited, when they throw over the jugs, and let them drift down stream. Then the party usually regales itself with a luncheon, after which the rowers start to pick up the floating jugs. Presently several of the jugs are seen to dive here and there, and the rowers follow them up until the fish become fatigued, and prone on their sides, they float on the surface of the stream, and are easily lifted into the boats. A catfish dinner and a hop usually winds up the day's recreation."

Fishing in American Waters
—Genio C. Scott, 1888

Sweet Fried Fillets

Personally I am not crazy about this one although a close friend and frequent fishing partner considers it delightful. For that reason I will reserve judgment until more people have a chance to try it and decide. Certainly not all taste buds are the same, thank goodness.

1. Put the fillets into a zip-lock bag and add the ginger ale.

2. Allow to soak for 2 to 4 hours, drain and rinse.

3. Mix all the dry ingredients in a bowl, making sure that you get them well blended.

4. Dip the fillets into the beaten egg and coat well with the dry mixture, then drop them into hot oil at 325 to 340 degrees.

Materials needed:

2 pounds of catfish fillets
(1) 12-ounce bottle ginger ale
1 cup crushed corn flakes
1/2 cup crushed
    Frosted Flakes
3 tablespoons flour
2 tablespoons oregano
1 tablespoons paprika
1/2 teaspoons ground cloves
1 egg, beaten

Double-Dipped Fillets

If you have ever eaten fish at a fast-food place you know about the crispy crust that many of them have as standard fare. That crunchy texture adds something different and a lot of people like it even if the spices used by the restaurant are not what they would prefer. There is a simple way to have it both ways, and the crust can be as thick or as thin as you like.

1. Blend the egg and milk; combine the cracker crumbs, cornmeal, salt and onion powder in a shaker bag.

2. Sprinkle the fillets with lemon juice or dip them in lemon juice and shake off excess.

3. Dip the fillets into the egg and milk mixture, then drop into the shaker bag and make sure that they are coated overall. If you want a thin crust, drop them into your cooker as is. For a thicker crust repeat the dipping and shaking process.

This recipe can be varied considerably since the crust is subject to all kinds of spice variations. I keep a wide variety of powdered peppers on hand and when my buddies who like spicy stuff are on hand, we experiment with cayenne, arbol chile, New Mexico, pasilla and various other peppers. Toss in some celery seeds and paprika for those who like spice without heat.

Materials needed:

Enough fillets to fry up for you
    and your guests
1 large lemon
1 egg
1 cup milk
2 cups finely crushed cracker crumbs
1 cup yellow cornmeal
2 tablespoons seasoned salt
Onion powder to taste,
    usually about 1 teaspoon

* For side dishes, do what the food places do and serve hush puppies, coleslaw and French fries.

More Crispy Fillets

When I first heard about this recipe, I almost became ill. That was quite a few years ago and I had trouble getting acquainted with yogurt because of the name: it just simply did not sound good. Luckily I eventually learned the error of my ways. Just remember to use the plain stuff because the kind with the fruit and stuff in it won't work.

1. Combine the yogurt and spices except for salt and pepper, mixing well.

2. Add the fillets and make sure that they are completely coated.

3. Cover the dish and refrigerate for at least an hour.

4. Combine the cornmeal with salt and pepper; dredge the fillets in the mixture.

5. Fry as usual at 325 to 340 degrees.

Materials needed:

4 to 6 catfish fillets
(1) 16-ounce carton of yogurt
1 to 2 teaspoons garlic powder, depending on taste
1 teaspoon paprika
2 cups cornmeal
Salt & pepper to taste

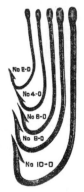

Instant Biology Lesson

More than 2,200 species of catfish swim the waters of the world, about eight percent of the total number of fishes. Catfish are found on every continent except Antarctica.

A catfish's whiskers, or barbels, are organs of taste and feel. They're sensitive to touch and covered with taste buds. Thus, they assist a catfish in finding food, even in muddy water. Some folks think the barbels can sting, but this is only a myth.

Perhaps the most amazing sense possessed by catfish is that of electroreception. Look closely on a catfish's head and along its lateral line and you'll notice small scattered pores. These are sensory organs that detect electrical fields in living organisms.

Davy's Deep-Fried Chunks

My old friend and sometimes cooking companion Davy Dennie refuses to deep-fry whole fish, or even steaks or fillets. He slices the meat into chunks of similar size, usually 2- to 3- inches squares by 1/2 to 1 inch in thickness. The chunks cook quickly and uniformly, plus he can add hush puppies and freshly sliced French fries as he goes rather than cooking in shifts.

1. Preheat the oil to 330 to 350 degrees.

2. Combine the cornmeal and spices in a bag and shake the freshly cut fish chunks for complete coverage.

3. Add French fries to the oil first since they will take longer to cook, then alternate with the fish chunks and hush puppies.

4. Fish will float when done. Fries will float before they are brown and crispy.

Materials needed:

Cooking pot
(4- to 6- quart minimum)
Slotted spoon
Oil to fill half of pot
White cornmeal
Salt, pepper and onion powder

Fish Munchies

This recipe is another way of deep-frying catfish, but one which produces a noticeably different end result. Rather than being a breading such as cornmeal, a batter is used. The batter is what results in flavor and texture alterations. In essence, the hot oil quickly turns the batter to a crispy crust while the fish inside steams and takes on characteristics of the spices used.

1. Cut the fish into chunks roughly 2 inches square by 1/2 to 1 inch thick. Dry the chunks and set aside on paper towels.

2. Combine egg, milk, flour, cornmeal, salt, pepper and other spices.

3. Grate 1/2 the onion, 1/2 the lemon, rind and all, and a enough of the bell pepper so that the volume equals that of the grated onion. Add to the batter and stir well.

4. Dredge the fish chunks in the batter and place in the preheated cooking pot. They will rise to the surface when done, but be sure to allow the crust to reach a rich brown, rolling them in the oil with the spoon to expose all surfaces.

5. Drain and serve.

Materials needed:

2 pounds catfish
Cooking pot
   (size can vary according to the
   amount being prepared)
Cooking oil (enough to half-fill pot)
Slotted spoon
1 egg
1/4 cup milk
1/3 cup flour
1/3 cup cornmeal
Salt & pepper
Chili powder, garlic powder
   or other spices (optional)
1 white onion
   (about the size of a tennis ball)
1 lemon
1 bell pepper

* Munchies go well with tartar or cocktail sauce, but ketchup or a ketchup-horseradish mix will work.

Two-Step Fish Munchies

The same basic steps and ingredients are used as in the previous recipe, but this recipe is unique in that it starts with boiled chunks of catfish, striper or even a large walleye. When the finished product comes from the cooker, challenge your guests to identify the type of seafood used. Some of the guesses may surprise you.

99 LBS.NET WEIGHT
WHOLE BEAN
UNCOATED
TABLE RICE

1. To prepare, follow the directions on 1 package of Zatarain's Shrimp and Crab Boil mix or a similar high-quality product. This particular brand is my favorite because of its spicy taste and consistent quality. Do as the instructions on the box say and you can't go wrong. Just make sure not to grossly overcook so that the pieces fall apart.

2. After removing the chunks from the boil, drain well and chill to near room temperature. You can even refrigerate overnight when planning a feed for the next day.

3. When cooking time rolls around, follow the basic recipe for Fish Munchies on the previous page.

Materials needed:

Zatarain's Shrimp & Crab Boil mix
Fish Munchies recipe on previous page

Whether or not you are planning to use these munchies for appetizers or as a main dish, keep some of the boiled chunks refrigerated until your family or guests are getting worked up over the cooking aromas. Serve the chilled chunks on toothpicks with bowls of cocktail sauce, tartar sauce and horseradish sauce.

* Incidentally, when selecting catfish for either hors d'oeuvres, appetizers, or any form of munchies, pick larger ones. Fish from 4 pounds upward have a "meatier" texture and are less likely to come apart in the spiced boil than pieces taken from small catfish. Cut with the grain as much as possible. You might also wish to boil the pieces in a cheesecloth bag, but personally I am too lazy to go to the trouble.

No Other Fish Will Do

"...the [man], who when fishing for catfish, was seen to catch a fine, large pickerel, deliberately take him off the hook, and throw him out into the stream as far as his strength would enable him to hurl him, and who, in answer to an inquiry as to his reason for so doing, replied:"I'se fishin' for catfish I is, an' when I fishes for cats I wants cats, an' dont want no pickerel to come foolin' aroun' my hook!"

Our Sister Republic
—Albert S. Evans, 1871

Roll 'Em Up Fillets

Hardly anyone thinks of fried fish as "pretty", but here is a recipe that really lends itself to some type of display. Garnish it brightly, arrange pieces in a circle around a large serving dish, use your imagination.

1. This recipe calls for fillets that have been scaled and the skin left on. Score the fillets from top to bottom at 1/2-inch intervals, being careful not to cut completely through. A scoring board that has grooves simplifies the process, but I have gotten by using a plastic plate.

2. Combine all the ingredients except the paprika in a bag or bowl with snug-fitting lid and mix well.

3. Shake the fillets, then put aside to let the breading "set" for about 5 minutes.

4. Stretch the fillets to open the scored areas and dust lightly with paprika.

5. Roll the fillets with the tail inside, then pin with a toothpick and dust the tops with paprika.

6. Fry at 330 to 350 degrees until brown and floating.

Materials needed:

Cooking pot
   (6-quart capacity or larger)
Slotted spoon
Scoring board
   (a cutting board will work)
2 pounds of Fish fillets
Salt & pepper
White cornmeal
Paprika

Traditional side dishes are fine here, but try a Caesar salad and bowls of assorted sauces. If this recipe strikes a responsive chord, follow the same basic procedure but baste the fillets with a mixture of mustard and prepared cayenne pepper before sprinkling on the paprika.

* I have had great success using this recipe for small bass, crappie, walleye, Spanish mackerel and even big bluegills.

A Man and His Fish

Last summer was so dry that the creek nearly ran dry. You could just about walk across it from bank to bank. Among the rocks, brush and such trash revealed by the low water were little pools jammed full of fish. As the weather got hotter and hotter the pools got smaller and the fish got desperate. One old boy who lived around those parts took pity on a big catfish that he found with its back sticking out of one of the mud holes. He took that big cat out of the water and taught it how to walk on its fins. It was a sight to see when that fish started following him around just like a dog. By the time the rains finally started and the creek filled back up, that catfish had gotten used to living on dry ground and for a while the sight of that old fellow and his catfish rambling around the countryside was the talk of the whole county. Well, one day the man showed up at the store without his fish. All the loafers on the porch wondered where it had got to — some even allowed as how they suspected that he'd eaten it. "Naw," said the man pulling a long face, "me and th' cat was a'walkin acrost the bridge down by the 'bandoned mill an' he slipped an' fell oft th' bridge and drowned!"

Traditional Southern Tall Tale

Catfish Cake

Here's a dish that I made a lot when my kids were young. I have made a few modifications along the way, which is the natural thing to do. The current version is one of the few fried fish recipes that lends itself to being served with biscuits and gravy rather than hush puppies. If you enjoy salmon patties give these a try—they're even better.

1. Place fillets, egg, onion and peppers in a food processor and chop thoroughly.

2. Mix flour and cornmeal.

3. Knead the fish mixture with the breading slowly, adding the flour-cornmeal mixture until the whole thing takes on a dough-like feel, then cover and refrigerate for an hour or more.

4. On waxed paper or other smooth surface spread the remainder of the flour-cornmeal mixture.

5. Pinch wads of the fish mixture about the size of a tennis ball and flatten into patties.

4. Lay patties in the flour-cornmeal mixture and sprinkle with celery seeds, salt and pepper. Coat both sides of the patties well.

6. Fry on top of the stove over medium or medium-high heat until golden brown. The outside edges should be crispy while the inside will be soft, moist and steamy.

Materials needed:

2 pounds of fillets
1 egg
1 medium onion
Fresh cayenne or
    jalapeño peppers to taste
1/2 cup flour
1/2 cup cornmeal
1/2 teaspoon celery seeds
Salt & pepper to taste

* Cook your fillets in shrimp and crab boil letting them sit long enough to take on as much of the flavor as possible, then proceed with the recipe above.

Trotline

A traditional fishing method used by both subsistence
and commercial catfishermen is the trotline. A
Trotline is a series of hooks on short lines tied to a
long cord at intervals of a couple of feet. The cord is
then tied to a tree trunk or bush on the riverbank and
drawn out into the river or pond. The fisherman can
bait the hooks and pull in the lines from the bank by
"trotting" along the shore. Trotlines are frequently left
overnight, with the fisherman returning in the early
morning to pull in his catch.

Cracker-Fried Fish

As mentioned earlier, breading choices can vary quite a bit, so this one should not be seen as an insult to my Georgia friends despite the name. For small fish, or anytime that you feel a change is in order, try using crushed crackers rather than cornmeal or flour. This produces a delicate coating that also adds crispness to the finished product. For those on a no-salt or low-salt diet, get the unsalted saltines, if you can imagine such a thing, and use a salt substitute.

1. For general cooking, simply sprinkle pepper and a small amount of onion powder onto the fish and dredge it in the cracker crumbs.

2. Slip it into the hot grease and proceed as usual. If, however, you want a really crispy, crunchy crust, remove the fish from the refrigerator or cooler, dry with paper towels, then dip in the milk and egg mixture.

3. Dredge the fish in crushed crackers, then dip and dredge a second time before putting the fish into the oil. The crust will seal the fish quickly and in effect you will be steam cooking the contents. The difference in taste and texture can be quite surprising.

Materials needed:

Large skillet or cooking pot
Spatula or tongs
8- to 12-inch whole fish
Pepper
Onion powder
Crackers, finely crushed
Salt (if necessary, or desired)
1 egg (optional)
1/4 cup milk (optional)
cooking oil

Cracker-crumb breading will burn more easily than cornmeal, so be careful with your heat. I prefer to preheat to 340 degrees, turn the fish as soon as the breading has "set," then lower the heat to 325 degrees. You may want to crank the temperature back up just before removing the fish to drain to produce a crispier end result.

Martha Washington's Fish Recipe

First set on yr water with pretty store of salt, 2 or 3
nutmegs quartered, & 2 or 3 ounions cut in halves.
When it boyls, put in ye fish on a plate, & against it
is enough, make yr sauce wth gravy, white wine, and
an anchovie or 2 melted in it. Put in store of butter
beaten up thick, barbaries, capers minced, pickled
cockls or oysters, a little juice of orring or leamon. yn
tayls up together as high as can in a large dish &
poure all ye sauce on ym & garnish yr dish leamon
sliced, barbaries, & capers.

Booke of Cookery
—Martha Washington, 1749

Mexi-Chunk Fish

This is another case where a breading makes a substantial difference in the finished product. I commonly prepare it as a sort of appetizer or as a snack item when a number of cooks (and diners) gather. Depending on your taste buds and durability, this dish can have one person practically weeping for joy and another weeping because he thinks his tongue has been permanently disabled. Feel free to add or subtract from the amount of peppers and spices given here.

1. In a food processor, finely chop 2 to 4 peppers. I normally use 2 of each, preferably right from the garden. Drop the onion in with them so that all three items are reduced to very small pieces.

2. Blend the milk and egg and add the pepper and onion mixture, chili powder, garlic powder, and salt and black pepper to taste.

3. With a sharp knife, cut the fillets, which have been dried on paper towels, into chunks like those used in Fish Munchies.

4. Dip the pieces into the pepper batter and drop them into oil which has been preheated to 330 to 350 degrees, or you can roll the battered chunks in a 50-50 mixture of cornmeal and flour. The latter is often done to surprise the unwary since it camouflages the pepper.

Materials needed:

Mixing bowl
Deep fryer or pot
Slotted spoon
2 pounds of Fish fillets
Cayenne pepper, fresh or frozen
Jalapeño pepper, fresh or frozen
1 small onion
1/4 cup milk
1 egg
1 tablespoon chili powder
1 teaspoon garlic powder
Salt & pepper
Cooking oil

Expect Mexi-Fish morsels to turn darker than other types of fried fish when cooking. This is because the pepper skins naturally do that, not because you are burning anything. When they float, roll them around a time or two, then remove from the oil to drain.

* Be forewarned that not all pieces will be the same. Some will get a heavier dose of the pepper heat than others because there is no way to make sure that the coating is even or uniform.

Catfish in the Straw

Met Mr. Catfish comin' down stream.
Says Mr. Catfish, "What does you mean?"
Caught Mr. Catfish by the snout,
And turned Mr. Catfish wrong side out.

Turkey in the straw, turkey in the hay,
Roll 'em up and twist 'em up a high tuckahaw
And twist 'em up a tune called Turkey in the Straw.

Turkey in the Straw
American popular tune 1834

Simple Fish Sticks

Another quick and easy method of frying produces what could best be called "finger food." The only problem here is that few pieces ever make it to the dining table. At a full-scale cooking with several buddies around, you also need to figure on more fish than normal as well as an adequate supply of stomach medication for those who overdo things a bit.

ABSOLUTELY
PURE

BOTTLED MILK

1. Mix the milk and egg in a bowl large enough to handle all the fillet strips.

2. Dry the strips on paper towels, then allow them to soak in the milk and egg mixture for 5 to 10 minutes.

3. Combine the other ingredients in a one-gallon freezer bag or similar container.

4. Remove strips from the liquid, drop them into a shaking bag and shake well.

5. Drop the strips into 350-degree oil and remove them when they pop to the top, nicely browned.

* Kids of all ages love this dish.

Materials needed:

Mixing bowl
Knife
Tongs or slotted spoon
Deep fryer or pot
2 pounds of fillets,
    cut into 1-inch strips
2 cups milk
1 egg
1/2 cup flour
1 ½ cups corn meal
Salt & pepper to taste
Onion powder and/or
    garlic powder are optional
Cooking oil

Cereal Breaded Fish

I have already mentioned the fact that saltine crackers work well as a breading material, but so do some other staple foods found in the kitchen. Back in the days when my two youngsters seemed like a small army and there were usually several of their friends around at mealtime, it was not unusual to have several boxes of breakfast cereal sitting around, opened, on the counters.

1. This is an easy one. While I prefer to dry my fillets, then dip them into the milk, it is actually quite feasible to forget the milk. Water will work in a pinch.

2. Whichever way you go, sprinkle salt and pepper on the fish, then dip the wet fillets in the crushed cereal flakes and drop them into hot oil.

Materials needed:

Deep fryer or cooker
2 pounds of fillets
Salt & pepper to taste
1/2 cup milk
2 cups finely crushed cereal flakes
Cooking oil

If you face a similar problem, this could help get rid of some of the leftovers while adding something different to your fish cooking repertoire. Any cereal except those with a sugar coating or fruit added will work, but those made from whole grain corn or wheat suit me best.

* Experiment until you find a favorite, then buy that brand and hide it from the depredations caused by hungry kids.

Potato Flake Fish

Anyone who has ever attended a fish fry knows that the versatile spud is a natural part of many meals. French fries are a staple, and once in a while someone gets inventive enough to put a bowl of potato salad on the table as an alternative.

1. Dip the fillets in the buttermilk or beer, salt and pepper, then dredge them in the dry ingredients.

2. Drop into 330 to 340-degree oil. Do not overcook—potato flakes can burn easily if the oil is too hot.

* Few folks have found that potato flakes, also known as instant potatoes, make an excellent and different breading material. Once again, it is a quick and easy product to use. I like to mix crushed crackers or corn flakes with mine on roughly a 50-50 mixture. Try it both ways and see what you like best.

Materials needed:

Deep fryer or pot
Tongs or slotted spoon
Mixing bowl
2 pounds of fillets
1 cup buttermilk
    (I sometimes substitute beer.)
Salt & pepper to taste
2 cups potato flakes or
    flake/cracker/cereal mix
Cooking oil

Huckleberry and Jim Catch a Whopper

"Well, the days went along, and the river went down between its banks
again; and about the first thing we done was to bait one of the big hooks
with a skinned rabbit and set it and catch a catfish that was as big as
a man, being six foot two inches long, and weighed over two hundred
pounds. We couldn't handle him, of course; he would a flung us into
Illinois. We just set there and watched him rip and tear around till he
drownded. We found a brass button in his stomach and a round ball,
and lots of rubbage. We split the ball open with the hatchet, and there
was a spool in it. Jim said he'd had it there a long time, to coat it over
so and make a ball of it. It was as big a fish as was ever catched in the
Mississippi, I reckon. Jim said he hadn't ever seen a bigger one. He
would a been worth a good deal over at the village. They peddle out such
a fish as that by the pound in the market-house there; everybody buys
some of him; his meat's as white as snow and makes a good fry."

The Adventures
of Huckleberry Finn
—Mark Twain, 1884

Sportfish Parmesan

This is another fried fish recipe that utilizes unsalted cracker crumbs and allows me to use beer as well. You will not need an entire bottle of brew, so dispose of the rest in an approved manner: drink it while you cook.

1. Combine the beer and egg.

2. Mix the dry ingredients in a plastic bag.

3. Dip the fillets in the beer and egg mixture, then shake them well in the cheesy breading in the plastic bag.

4. You can deep-fry the fillets, but this breading will take its toll on the oil quickly. In a skillet, use about 1/4 inch of oil and cook at 350 degrees for 3 to 5 minutes per side.

5. Drain and serve.

Materials needed:

Large skillet, preferably cast iron
2 pounds of fillets
1/2 cup beer
1 medium egg
2 cups crushed crackers
1/4 cup Parmesan cheese
   (the sprinkle type from a can)
1 teaspoon oregano or
   Italian seasoning
Salt & pepper to taste
Cooking oil

If you really love spicy foods, this is a dish that can practically be turned into a sort of "mini-pizza" with catfish involved. This is the basic recipe; experiment with my blessing.

* Try a salad and bread-sticks on the side. Just make sure that you have plenty because the aroma of these fish cooking will have mouths watering.

World Giants

The wels, or Danubian catfish (Silurus glanis) is widespread in Europe from southern Sweden southward to the Alps and as far eastward as the Sea of Aral. The wels inhabits rivers, lakes, and reservoirs and the enormous fish has also been introduced into England, France, Spain, and Italy. One of the largest freshwater fish, wels have been known to reach a length of 9 feet 10 inches and a weight of more than 400 pounds. A predatory species, the wels will eat just about everything. Introduced in Great Britain in the 1870's and 1880's, it is thought by some that one of the large houses around Loch Ness may have stocked the catfish in their private lake. One or more might have escaped into the loch and sightings of the enormous fish may be the origin of the Loch Ness Monster.

Monster catfish also dwell in the Amazon and its tributaries. The most spectacular is the piraiba (Brachyplatystoma filamentosum), which is said to reach sizes of 10 feet long and weigh in excess of 500 pounds. Local fishermen catch them by baiting huge hooks with beef hearts and attaching the hooks to floats with nylon rope. The floats are allowed to drift down the deep main channels of the river and the fisherman follows in a canoe. Tales abound of piraiba turning

continued on page 40

Italian Seasoned Fish

Since the previous recipe reminds me somewhat of pizza, it is only fair to follow it up with another spicy dish that smells just about as good. I call it "Italian Seasoned" simply because the words are easy to spell and it once again gives off the aroma so familiar to a good pasta restaurant. It was almost called "Crouton Catfish," but I don't know how to spell "crouton."

1. Crush the croutons finely and add the flour, oregano salt and pepper. Mix well and put into a shaking bag.

2. Whip the egg whites. You may add 1/4 cup of milk if you like.

3. Dry the fillets, dip in the egg whites, then shake them well in breading.

4. Drop the fillets into 350-degree oil. Pay attention. The breading mixture with the egg whites seals the meat, steaming it and cooking it quickly. Take care not to overcook.

Materials needed:

Deep fryer or pot
Tongs
2 pounds of fillets
1 box onion & garlic croutons
1/2 cup flour
1/2 teaspoon oregano
Salt & pepper to taste
Whites from 4 medium-eggs

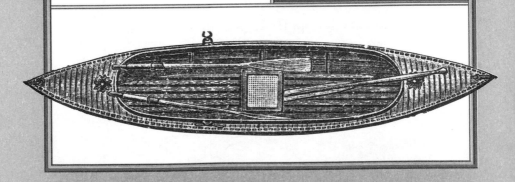

the table is evidenced by wrecked boats and missing fishermen. Another formidable Amazonian species is the reel-emptying redtail catfish (Phractocephalus hemioliopterus). The world record is 97 pounds. When caught, the redtail emits a series of loud grunts, squeals and gurgles as it approaches the boat.

The title of the world's largest confirmed catfish is held by the Giant Mekong catfish (Pangasianodon gigas), called the pla buk in Thai. The endangered giant inhabits large rivers from India to its spawning grounds in the Mekong River system. It shows one of the fastest growth rates of any fish in the world. The Mekong can weigh as much as 650 pounds and measure up to 10 feet in length. They are the largest scaleless freshwater fish in the world.

Picante Fish

If you like spicy dishes, but not necessarily hot ones, then this is something that you should try. It revolves around a dip made from commercial or homemade picante sauce, so you get to control the degree of external heat applied. This is a great "add and subtract" recipe as well. One of my friends cannot stand the taste of celery so he substitutes oregano. Feel free to go even farther afield if your tastes take you that way.

1. Combine all the dry ingredients and blend well in a freezer bag or other vessel while melting 1 stick of butter at medium-high heat in your skillet. You will add the other stick a little at a time as needed.

2. Mix the egg whites and milk.

3. Dry the fillets, then dip them thoroughly in the milk and egg mixture.

4. Drop the filletsinto the seasoning bag and shake well, then cook for 4 to 5 minutes per side or until brown on the outside and flaky on the inside. Drain on paper towels.

5. Mix the picante sauce, lemon juice and horseradish and use for a dip in place of cocktail or tartar sauce.

Materials needed:

Large skillet, cast iron preferred
2 to 3 pounds of fillets
1 cup yellow cornmeal
1 teaspoon garlic powder
1 teaspoon onion powder
1 teaspoon celery seeds
2 sticks butter
2 egg whites, beaten
1/4 cup milk
Small jar picante sauce
Juice from 1 lemon
2 tablespoons prepared horseradish

*This is a good multi-option dish since you can use more than one heat level of sauce to please different taste buds.

Teddy's Cat

"We spent a day... determining our exact position by the sun, and afterward by the stars, and sending on two men to explore the rapids in advance. They returned with the news that there were big cataracts in them, and that they would form an obstacle to our progress. They had also caught a huge iluroid fish, which furnished an excellent meal for everybody in camp. This evening at sunset the view across he broad river, from our camp where the two rivers joined, was very lovely; and for the first time we had an open space in front of and above us, so that after nightfall the stars, and the great waxing moon, were glorious over-head, and against the rocks in midstream the broken water gleamed like tossing silver.

The huge catfish which the men had caught was over three feet and a half long, with the usual enormous head, out of all proportions to the body, and the enormous mouth, out of all proportion to the head. Such fish, although their teeth are small, swallow very large prey. This one contained the nearly digested remains of a monkey. Probably the monkey had been seized while drinking from the end of a branch; and once engulfed in that yawning cavern there was no escape. We Americans were astounded at the idea of

continued on page 44

Stir-Fry Fish

My fishing partner Dave Dennie is something of a stir-fry nut. He even has a specially, made wok that is just one size smaller than a military Quonset hut in which he does his cooking. When he offers to prepare this dish, I play dumb and stay out of the kitchen. The knives that he uses are sharp enough to scare a pirate, and one of these days I'm sure that a part of him will wind up in the entrée.

1. Cut the fish into 1-inch chunks or strips.

2. Mix the strips with the cornstarch until coated.

3. Combine all the liquid ingredients plus salt, pepper and garlic powder and refrigerate for 30 minutes.

4. In the wok or pot, add the 1/4 cup of oil, then the broccoli, cauliflower, onion and carrots. Cook at medium heat for about 3 to 4 minutes.

5. Add a can of prepared Oriental vegetables or water chestnuts if you would like.

6. Stir in the marinade, fish and mushrooms and cook an additional 5 to 7 minutes or until the fish flakes easily.

Materials needed:

Wok or similar large cooking vessel
1 1/2 pounds of fish, preferably taken from steaks off a large (5-pound plus) fish. The meaty texture is an asset.
Cornstarch
1/4 cup teriyaki sauce
Splash of vegetable oil (2 to 3 tablespoons)
Juice of 1/2 lemon
Salt & pepper to taste
1/4 teaspoon garlic powder
1/4 cup vegetable oil
1 cup broccoli
1 cup cauliflower
1/2 cup chopped green onions
1 cup sliced carrots
1 cup sliced mushrooms

*
I have also prepared this dish in a neat wok/grill combo intended for outdoor use. It is called the "Waco Wok" and is made from agricultural disc blades. Check with major hardware supply houses since I have no idea how to obtain a new one. Mine was a gift from a friend who forgot to tell his wife that he had left the "WW" in the garage. It made an impressive dent on the hood of her car, especially the scratch where the blade rolled all the way across. Use and store with caution.

a catfish making prey of a monkey; but our Brazilian friends told us that in the lower Madeira and the part of the Amazon near its mouth there is a still more gigantic catfish which in similar fashion occasionally makes prey of man. This is a grayish-white fish over nine feet long, with the usual disproportionately large head and gaping mouth... It is called the piraiba...

While stationed at the small city of Itacoatiara, on the Amazon, at the mouth of the Madeira, the doctor had seen one of these monsters which had been killed by the two men it had attacked. They were fishing in a canoe when it rose from the bottom... and raising itself half out of the water lunged over the edge of the canoe at them, with open mouth. They killed it with their falcóns, as machetes are called in Brazil. It was taken round the city in triumph in an oxcart; the doctor saw it, and said it was three metres long. He said that swimmers feared it even more than the big cayman, because they could see the latter, whereas the former lay hid at the bottom of the water. Colonel Rondon said that in many villages where he had been on the lower Madeira the people had built stockaded enclosures in the water in which they bathed, not venturing to swim in the open water for fear of the piraiba and the big cayman."

Through the Brazilian Wilderness
—Theodore Roosevelt, 1914

Vino Fried Fish

Cooking with potable liquids, especially wine, has been going on for generations. From the looks of some European menus, it would appear that meat, fish and fowl only come to the table in a soused condition but they taste wonderful.

1. Mix all the marinade ingredients except the wine in a pan and bring to a low boil. Stir to prevent burning.

2. Add the wine and allow to simmer for 5 to 10 minutes.

3. Remove from heat and divide into a shallow pan for marinating and a deep bowl for dipping.

4. Refrigerate. When cool, add the fillet strips to the marinade. Allow to sit for at least 2 hours.

5. Combine the milk and egg in a shallow pan or dish and combine the dry ingredients in another pan or shaking bag.

6. Remove the fillet strips from the marinade, dip them in the milk and egg mixture, and then shake in the breading.

7. Remove from the breading, dip in the milk and egg again, then back into the breading.

8. Fry in 330 to 350-degree oil, drain, then serve with the remainder of the dip/marinade mixture.

Materials needed:

Deep fryer or pot
(a large skillet will also work)
2 pounds of fillets, cut into 1-inch strips
1 cup flour
2 cups cornmeal
1 egg
1/2 cup milk
Salt & pepper to taste

Marinade/dip:
1 cup red wine
(I prefer a hearty Burgundy or Merlot.)
1 cup ketchup
2 tablespoons Dale's Steak Sauce
3 tablespoons brown sugar
1 tablespoon prepared horseradish
1/2 lemon, grated

A glass of the remaining wine will help round out the meal, and don't worry about the old saw about "only white wine with fish." If anyone complains, don't invite them back.

* Applying the use of wine to fish cooking is simple. In this case it serves as a sort of dip and marinade.

A Record Catch in Anybody's Book

Peter Pond was born in Milford, Connecticut, sometime around 1739. In 1765, after serving in the army, he joined his father in Detroit to work as a fur trapper. While trapping along the Illinois River, Pond set a trotline to catch fish to feed the men in his company.

"We put our hook and lines into the water and let them lie all night. In the morning we perceived that there was fish at the hooks and hauled on our line. At length we had one ashore that weighed a hundred and four pounds, a second that weighed one hundred pounds and a third of seventy-five pounds. The men were glad to see this for they had not ate meat for some days or fish for a long time... The fish was what was called a catfish. It had a large flat head sixteen inches long between the eyes."

"Journal of Peter Pond,"
Wisconsin Historical Collections

Pepper & Wine Fillets

This is another recipe passed along by a friend with whom I have spent a fair amount of time on the water. To the general public and those with whom he shares a newspaper office he seems somewhat eccentric. Actually he is not such a weird bird, but he does love to keep everyone wondering what he will pull next. For all of that, he is one of the finest cooks around. This one I owe to "The Sloan."

1. Soak the fillets in buttermilk for 2 hours or more. Keep refrigerated.

2. In your skillet, sauté the pepper strips and onion in just enough olive oil to get the job done. When slightly crisp, put them in a separate vessel atop the stove to stay warm.

3. Now combine the bread crumbs, cheese and other spices, no wine, dip the fillets in egg and dredge well.

4. Pour a couple of tablespoons of olive oil into your skillet, crank the heat up to medium high, and carefully place the fish into the oil.

5. Cook for about 5 minutes or until the fish have browned on one side, then pour in half of the wine around the edges of the skillet.

6. Turn the fillets, continue cooking and add wine as necessary. Normal cooking time is generally 10 to 12 minutes total, depending on the thickness of the fillets.

Materials needed:

Large skillet, cast iron preferred
2 pounds of fish fillets
Top-quality virgin olive oil
Sweet peppers, cut into strips
    (Italian, bell, banana, etc. Try different colors just to dress things up.)
1 large onion, red or white, sliced
4 to 6 eggs, well beaten
1 cup white wine, Chablis or Sauterne
1/4 prepared grated Parmesan cheese
Dash of garlic powder
1 tablespoon lemon pepper
Buttermilk
1½ cups bread crumbs

* "The Sloan" serves this fish dinner with the peppers, a buttered pasta and green salad with olive oil and vinegar dressing. It is truly worth the time and trouble.

Catfish I Q

A study done by Missouri fisheries biologist and river management expert Gordon B. Farabee tested the comparative learning ability of fish in three categories. Catfish learned quickest and achieved the highest overall scores, far above other popular sportfish like large-mouth and smallmouth bass, rainbow trout, northern pike and bluegill. Some catfish also seem to possess the ability to predict future events. For centuries the Chinese have used catfish to warn of earthquakes. When the fish become unnaturally active, there may be an earthquake on the way. In fact some catfish species are sensitive to low-frequency vibrations and can detect rumblings beneath the earth's crust days in advance.

Bettie's Beer Batter Method

Having mentioned my amigo Dave Dennie's cooking technique, it would be remiss of me not to include one preferred by his ever-patient spouse, Bettie. She insists that only dark beer will impart the proper taste, but I believe that she uses it simply because she knows that neither Dave nor I will drink the heavy stuff before she can use it in her cooking. Beer that is not good enough for spectators at a baseball game is not good enough for us.

1. Mix all the ingredients except the fish and stir thoroughly.

2. Dip the fish in the batter and drop it into hot oil. I prefer a temperature of about 350 to 375 degrees for this recipe—you do not want an oily crust.

3. When the fish bob to the top, roll to get all sides nicely browned; drain first in the basket, then on paper towels and serve.

Materials needed:

Deep fryer with wire or
  slotted basket
2 to 3 pounds of fillets
(2) 12-ounce bottles of dark beer,
  any brand
1½ cups self-rising flour
2 cups yellow cornmeal
4 egg whites
1 small onion, puréed
3 tablespoons prepared dry
  Italian seasoning
Cooking oil

GRILLING FACTS

The first fish ever cooked probably received some sort of grilling, if you could call it that. I suspect that it was simply tossed onto a fire and roasted until all appendages had been reduced to charred stumps. Meat closest to the skin was conceivably a tad overdone while the inner cuts might have exhibited some chewy characteristics.

Having tried, as a youth, to successfully cook a fish over an open fire without the benefit of any sort of grilling rack, I can sympathize with our distant ancestors in that long ago age. Never in all my attempts did I manage to keep even a dinky little catfish, perch or other specimen on my well-selected stick long enough to render it anything like truly edible. Only an adventurous, and very young, person would have kept trying to cook his catch. Only one whose brain had not benefited from a reality attack would have actually eaten those charred/raw monstrosities.

Notes on Grilling

1. If using charcoal (I use a Brinkmann Smoke 'N' Grill), fill the pan about half full of a quality charcoal such as Kingsford or Brinkmann. Cheaper products do not always burn easily and cleanly and may not last as long. Good charcoal gives consistent results, so find a favorite brand and stay with it. Doing anything else is like changing stoves every time you cook.

2. Light the charcoal and allow it to become an even, uniform gray on top before placing the rack with the fish on top. Put the lid in place and let the smoky heat do its thing. With fillets, 15 minutes is plenty unless they are overly thick, and 30 minutes should handle even a whole 3-pounder. The meat will flake easily when done.

3. Try not to overcook since this contributes to unnecessary dryness. Grilled fish is perhaps a little more elegant than most traditional recipes, so plan your vegetable selection accordingly. A glass of Chablis would not be amiss if served with the more flashy dishes.

Catfish Dogs

I got a team of the best waterdogs that anyone has
ever seen in this state. I raised 'em up from mudpup-
pys. They can pull a 20-foot flatboat so I don't need
no motor. When I'm not using them waterdogs to pull
the boat, I hunt catfish with 'em. I trained one pair to
chase an' tree catfish. One night they run a great big
old blue cat up a really tall sycamore tree. That cat
must have weighed over 700 pounds. When I shot the
catfish out of the tree, that fish fell about 100 feet
landed on both of them dogs, so help me, and it drove
them down into the river mud and I could never find
them. I did try to get the Army Engineers to build me
a coffer dam to get those dogs out, but nothin' ever
come of it. If you want to try, I marked the spot...
you can keep them dogs if you find them.

Southern "brag"

Lemon Grilled Catfish

This is another catfish recipe that will really be appreciated by anyone trying to cut down on oils and fats in their diet. It is also a fine recipe for those days when you prefer to grill outside rather than hang around in a hot kitchen, and the finished product is just as tasty as it is easy to cook.

1. Tear off enough aluminum foil to nearly cover the grill rack. Crimp it around the edges, then use a fork or knife to poke holes through the foil. Make plenty, since this allows oils and fats to cook away and make smoke upon hitting the hot surface below. Spray well with nonstick cooking oil spray.

2. Drain the fish thoroughly, place on the rack and sprinkle with salt and pepper to taste.

3. Place thin slices of onion completely over the fish, then top with a row of lemon slices down the center. Some cooks like to sprinkle a little soy sauce on top of the onion prior to adding the lemon, so feel free to do it either way.

Materials needed:

Grill (charcoal, gas or electric)
Fillets or whole fish
   (3 pounds and under)
Aluminum foil
Nonstick cooking oil spray
Salt & pepper
White onions
Lemons

Italian Marinade Magic

Italian dressing, either the regular or low-fat version, makes an excellent marinade for all types of meat and fish. If you decide to use it—and I recommend it—drain the fillets or whole fish. Then put them into a one-gallon freezer bag along with about half a bottle of olive oil-based dressing and swish them around occasionally for at least an hour prior to cooking time.

The cooking procedure is identical to that given for Lemon Grilled Catfish, but you will need to remove the grill cover every 5 minutes or so to baste with the remaining dressing marinade. If you are using fillets, you might have guests try and guess what species of fish they are eating.

Campfire Grilled Fish

This simple and delicious recipe came from fixing meals while fishing in out-of-the-way places. It has also proven quite popular for shore lunches. You can carry everything needed to prepare it in a corner of a backpack or a small storage area on a boat. Since it does not require constant attention, you can fix it in the oven while handling necessary chores such as cleaning the kitchen or watching your favorite television show.

1. Sprinkle salt and pepper to taste on the fillets.

2. Put a slice of onion on the foil, lay a fillet on top and then add a layer of pepper rings. Add lemon juice if you like.

3. Place a second piece of foil on top and fold both pieces together carefully to make a tight seal. This will hold in the juices.

4. If you prefer to use a grill rack, place the foil-wrapped fish on top.

5. With a campfire, simply keep your edibles in a small bed of coals or near a hotter pile. Turn often in either case. Do not rush this recipe; relax and let the packages cook for at least 30 minutes. If the fillets or vegetable slices are thick, make it 45 minutes.

Materials needed:

2 fillets per person, preferably from fish weighing less than 2 pounds
1 onion, red or white preferred
1 bell pepper
lemon (optional)
Salt & pepper
Aluminum foil

When cooking this combination at home, you may wish to experiment with butter, a commercial cooking sauce or even other spices.

*
Plain or fancy, it is a recipe that you will use more than once.

Campfire Fish *2

Here is another recipe that works well at streamside and that is actually where I found it. The late "Toad" Smith, an outdoor writer, former player in the National Football League and catfish angler extraordinaire related it to me on the banks of the Big South Fork of the Cumberland River several years ago. I still can't believe that the cloth does not burn; I suspect it has to be some sort of Midwestern magic.

1. Lay the cheesecloth out on a flat surface and put a fillet that has been sprinkled with salt and pepper on top.

2. Add a layer of onions, then another fillet.

3. Salt and pepper it, then wrap the "sandwich" in cheesecloth.

4. Baste well with the dressing or margarine and place on a grill or rack above the coals.

5. Cook for 5 minutes, basting often, then turn. Repeat the process 2 or 3 times depending on the thickness of the fillets and how well done you like your onions.

Materials needed:

2 catfish (or other lean fish) fillets per person
Italian salad dressing or plain old margarine in a squeeze bottle
1 onion (a big one, white or red)
Salt & pepper
Cheesecloth

* This is a dish that I normally cook alone beside the water, sort of a tribute to the memory of one of the world's great characters and a darned fine angler.

The Channel Catfish

"...in the upper Missouri River, where they are regard-
ed as superior to any other fish, the trout included,
[channel catfish] attain to fifteen pounds, and even
more. It is there called by some the lady-cat, because
of its great beauty and symmetry, while it is as active
as any fish known; and, on landing it, the fish croaks:
hence it is known by some as the croaker... The channel cat offers as good play as the trout, and when
angled for with fine tackle the sport is unsurpassed.
He makes the reel hum; and if the line is not kept clear
on the reel and the fish played gingerly, so as to make
him contend for every foot of line, he is quite sure to
part tackle."

Fishing in American Waters
—Genio C. Scott, 1888

Fancy Grilled Fish

You can use this recipe outside on the grill or inside in the oven. That makes it convenient for the occasions when you have a hankering for some low-calorie catfish but the weather makes outdoor grilling a less than viable option.

1. Mix all the ingredients except the catfish and place in a large bowl or one-gallon plastic freezer bag. I prefer the latter since it can be tossed into the garbage instead of being washed later.

2. Add the fish and refrigerate for a couple of hours, turning occasionally.

3. If you are grilling, toss a few apple, hickory or mesquite chips onto the coals just before adding the fillets. Apple chips are the personal favorite due to the pleasant bouquet that they impart to the whole affair.

4. On the grill or in the oven, give them about 4 to 5 minutes per side until they flake easily.

Materials needed:

2 to 3 pounds of catfish fillets
Juice from 2 lemons
1/4 cup finely chopped onion
1/4 cup soy sauce or
    Worcestershire sauce
1 teaspoon paprika
2 jalapeño or cayenne peppers,
    puréed
4 cloves garlic, puréed

"Along the Sides Were Great Spines"

The Gentleman of Elvas, an unidentified conquistador who chronicled Hernando DeSoto's 1539 expedition encountered catfish, that he identified as "bagre," in the Mississippi River near the mouth of the Arkansas.

"Where the Governor stayed was a great lake, near to the enclosure; and the water entered a ditch that well-nigh went round the town. From the River Grande to the lake was a canal, through which the fish came into it, and where the Chief kept them for his eating and pastime. With nets that were found in the place, as many were taken as need required; and however much might be the casting, there was never any lack of them ... The greater number differ from those in the fresh water of Spain. There was a fish called bagre, the third part of which was head, with gills from end to end, and along the sides were great spines, like very sharp awls ... in the river were some that weighed from one hundred to one hundred and fifty pounds."

True Relation of the Discovery
of the Province of Florida
—The Gentleman of Elvas, 1557

"Sour Mash" Fish

Since some of the best fishing is found where much of the world's best bourbon whiskey is made (and consumed), it is only natural that the two have been combined in cooking. Do not be deceived into thinking that the addition of bourbon will ruin the delicate flavor of your fish. It and the other spices and additives will only make it somewhat different from the norm. Just be sure not to get carried away and try to get rid of all the "leftovers" at one time.

1. A food processor is a great help with this recipe since it will reduce the garlic and citrus to very small particles. If you do not have one, borrow one from a friend.

2. Put everything except the fish into the processor and let it run until the items are well blended. It is a good idea to make this marinade early in the morning when your taste buds balk at the thought of a snort of whiskey and besides, the fillets need to sit in it for at least 8 hours. Preparing it the night before can be hazardous, resulting in a red-eyed tomorrow. Fillets and marinade can sit in a glass bowl or plastic freezer bag.

3. Over medium heat, put the fillets on the grill rack and baste often. Cook until they flake easily, usually 10 to 12 minutes total.

Materials needed:

3 to 4 pounds of catfish fillets
    (or other lean fish)
1 pint bourbon
2 lemons with seeds removed
1 orange with seeds removed
2 cloves garlic, peeled
1 tablespoon horseradish
1 teaspoon oregano or
    dry Italian seasoning

* Be sure not to approach the finished product with any preconceived ideas concerning the taste. Not even the most devout teetotaler or what W.C. Fields referred to as a "bluenose" will believe that a heady potion was used in the preparation.

How the Catfish Got the Way He Is

An old chief of the catfish once called all his people together by the waters edge and said to them, "Many times I have seen a moose come down into our lake to eat marsh grass. He always comes at the same time, when the sun rises a little way up in the sky. Together there are enough of us that we can kill the moose and eat him."

The catfish that heard this agreed to help kill the moose and hid themselves in the grass and cane near the shore. Just as the chief catfish had said, when the sun was a little way up in the sky, the moose came slowly along and waded down into the shallows, where he began to feed. At first the catfish were afraid because the moose was so big, but finally the old chief catfish swam through the reeds and thrust his spear into the moose's leg. Then the moose said, "What is it that has thrust a spear into my leg?"

When he saw all the catfish around his legs, he began to trample on them, killing many of them with his great hoofs and trampling others down into the soft mud. The terrified catfish that lived swam away down the river as fast as they could. To this day the catfish still carry their little spears, but their heads have never recovered from the flattening they received when they were trampled by the angry moose.

Menominee Oral Tradition

Wine & Sugar Fish

Here is a neat recipe using some unusual ingredients including wine, which imparts a sort of Continental flavor to fish. My old angling pal David Lawrence sprang this one on me a couple of years ago and I had to hold him over the grill to get him to give up the secret.

1. Melt the butter in a skillet or saucepan, then add the brown sugar, stirring until it is dissolved.

2. Add lemon juice and wine and let simmer over low heat for a few minutes. I occasionally sneak in a shot of soy sauce too, although the original recipe does not call for it.

3. Salt and pepper the fillets, baste them well, then place over medium coals and put the lid on your grill. Do not turn the fillets while cooking, since they come apart easily.

4. Cook for 6 to 10 minutes, possibly more if using thick fillets, basting as you go. When they flake easily they are ready to meet the wine at the table.

Materials needed:

2 pounds of fillets
White wine
  (You only need 1 tablespoon, so get something that you like on the table as well. A good Chablis or Sauterne suites me fine.)
2 sticks butter
2/3 cup brown sugar
Juice from 1 large lemon
Salt & pepper to taste

A Visitor to Kansas

"During the excessive drowth, a huge cat-fish (identical in appearance with the New England horned pout, which in its native streams seldom reaches the weight of one pound) came swimming down the river [Kansas River]. Just opposite Lecompton, the luckless voyager struck a sand-baron which he landed high and dry. He was captured by hand, and found to weigh one hundred and seventeen pounds. There was one afterward caught in the Missouri, weighing one hundred and sixty pounds. But the former demonstrated that the Kansas is not navigable for catfish in low water."

Beyond the Mississippi
—Albert Deane, 1869

One-Dish Grilled Meal

Fish and potatoes are traditional partners, so try fixing them together— literally. This is a true one-dish meal that can remain basic if you're camping in the back country, or you can dress it up at home.

1. Prepare baked potatoes on the grill, in the oven or microwave. The method does not matter. Cut in half and allow to cool.

2. Put each half in aluminum foil, put a fillet on top and add a generous pat of butter, a slice of white or purple onion, a dribble of fresh lemon juice and salt and pepper to taste.

3. Wrap tightly in foil and drop the packages on the grill. Fish is done when flesh flakes easily.

Materials needed:

2 fillets per person (minimum)
1 baking potato per person
Butter
Onion (white or purple)
Lemon
Salt & pepper

* It also works well in the oven, and fish such as big bluegill, crappie and small bass are naturals for this one. You can also trim big fillets to fit if you never catch anything small.

Tons of Okeechobee Cats

Between the turn of the twentieth century and World
War II, Florida's Lake Okeechobee, in the heart of the
Everglades, was the site of a major commercial catfish
industry. In 1924 alone, the fish camps around the
lake caught and shipped an estimated 6,500,000
pounds of fresh processed Channel, Yellow, Spotted
and Mud Cats. The fish were estimated to be worth
nearly one million dollars. The filleted fish were packed
in ice in 200-pound barrels and shipped via the
Indian Prairie Canal or later by railroad.

Limed Catfish

This dish, like many others, can be prepared on the grill or in the oven. Let your preference and the weather dictate which way you decide to go. This distinctively different recipe makes a great meat option for large dinner parties, whether they're formal or otherwise.

1. On a disposable baking pan or heavy foil well sprayed with nonstick cooking oil, lay the fillets.

2. Sprinkle each with lime juice.

3. Combine the lime peel and all the spices except the parsley with the butter or olive oil and spread half of the mixture over the fillets.

4. When the cooking is half over (about 3 to 4 minutes under the oven's broiler, 8 to 10 minutes on the grill), spread the remainder over the fillets and finish cooking. Sprinkle with parsley and serve.

Materials needed:

2 pounds Catfish fillets
1/2 cup melted butter or olive oil
1 teaspoon grated lime peel
Juice from 1 lime
1/2 teaspoon ground ginger
2 tablespoons chopped parsley
1/2 tablespoon cilantro
Salt & pepper to taste

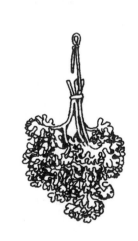

Grilled Cats & Corn

This dish is one that has become something of a personal tradition when doing an overnight run down one of the small rivers here in my native Southeast. Since there is room in a canoe or small flat-bottomed boat for a few extras (I don't do backpacks anymore), these allow you to pamper yourself and impress your companions. If you happen to live in a place where catfish mysteriously do not live, it is possible to substitute pretty much whatever swims there. You can even use trout although I hope you don't have to.

1. In a plastic freezer bag, marinade the catfish. Put it in the cooler for at least 2 hours. Remove, drain, and place each fish or fillet on a piece of foil.

2. Dust the fish with lemon pepper and seasoned salt. Wrap loosely and secure the ends to prevent leaks.

3. Rub ears of corn with margarine and season, then push the husks back into place and wrap in foil.

4. Grill for 10 minutes per side. Cooking time will vary depending on the size of the fish. Small ones and fillets, as well as the corn, require about 20 minutes total.

Materials needed:

2 small whole catfish,
   (1) 3-pounder, or appropriate
   number of fillets per person
Small bottle zesty Italian dressing
Lemon pepper
Seasoned salt
Margarine
Fresh corn with silks removed
Heavy-duty aluminum foil

Bacon Grilled Goodies

While I readily admit to loving any sort of good beef cut wrapped in bacon prior to grilling, I must as quickly state that doing the same with fish can be a bit frustrating. It can also be delicious if you are willing to take the time to do it right. Unlike beef, freshwater fish must be cooked thoroughly to be safe and you can encounter a situation where the bacon is crispy, possibly incinerated, but the fish is not quite done.

1. Season each fillet before wrapping with bacon and pinning with toothpicks. A drip pan can be used (certainly use one in the oven if that is where you are cooking), but I like the smoky taste the drippings impart on the charcoal. The solution is a low fire and frequent turnings.

2. Have a spray bottle of water on hand to take care of sudden conflagrations.

Materials needed:

2 pounds Catfish Fillets
Thick bacon
Round toothpicks
Salt & pepper to taste
Onion powder or garlic powder
  (optional)

Flatheads

Flathead catfish grow faster than any other North
American game fish. The fastest growth spurt typically
occurs between ages three and eight when they
commonly add two to five pounds per year. Even
big flats can gain more than 10 pounds annually.
Nicknames for flatheads are legion. Those commonly
heard include yellow cat, shovelhead, mud cat, Morgan
cat, appaloosa cat, appaluchion, johnnie cat, goujon,
Opelousas cat, Op cat, bashaw, Russian cat, granny
cat, pied cat, flatbelly and Mississippi cat.

Grilled Catfish with Garden Vegetables

This is a great addition to any outdoor fish cooking when you have friends around. On many occasions I pick the vegetables right on the spot while my buddy heats up the oil for traditional fried catfish. This is an easy and fun dish that looks nice, too.

1. Oil the pan, put in the fillets and sprinkle with oil.

2. Finely chop the onion or run it through a food processor.

3. Peel the tomatoes and chop them, then combine them with the onion in the same container.

4. Spread the tomato and onion mixture over the fillets and sprinkle the spices according to taste over the top.

5. Put the fillets into the pan over a medium flame or charcoal. Cook uncovered for 15 to 20 minutes. Whenever the fish flakes easily, it is done.

Materials needed:

Disposable aluminum baking pan
Enough fillets to fill the pan
    without overlapping
Olive oil
1 large sweet onion
2 or 3 fresh tomatoes
Celery seed
Basil
Paprika
Salt & pepper

*For a different variation, poke holes in the bottom of the pan and cover during the last 5 minutes or so. This adds a smoky touch that some people like yours truly prefer.

Teriyaki Grilled Kabobs

Here is an incentive for you to keep an occasional fish that is too large for your skillet. You need one weighing at least 5 pounds and 10 or more is better because larger fish do not fall apart so badly on the grill. My favorite is a flathead of about the aforementioned size. I've also prepared this dish using blue cats weighing over 40 pounds and nobody complained. Just be sure not to include any of the reddish meat that runs down the side of the fish or your end product may have too much of a fishy taste to garner any compliments.

1. Combine all the ingredients in a one-gallon freezer bag and marinade for at least 30 minutes.

2. Arrange on wooden skewers, which have been soaked overnight to prevent scorching, in an alternating manner: catfish chunk, pineapple, pepper, mushroom, more fish, etc. There is no wrong way to do it, and you might even want to try some rings of jalapeño peppers just to add more spice.

3. Dust with seasoned salt and lemon pepper prior to putting on the grill.

4. Figure about 5 minutes over the charcoal, turning and basting at least once. If the fish chunks start to break apart, you are overcooking.

Materials needed:

Teriyaki marinade
  (I use Lawry's with pineapple juice)
30 to 40 strips of catfish fillet,
  roughly 1/2 inch by 1/2 inch
  by 1 1/2 inches
1 can pineapple chunks
Red and green bell peppers,
  cut into strips
1 pound large mushrooms
  with caps removed
Seasoned salt and
  lemon pepper to taste

Grilled Fish with Garden Stuff

During the warm months, I enjoy items from the garden as much as I enjoy properly cooked fish. You can also buy the veggies if you like, but by all means try this different and tasty meal. It is also a nice treat for those who have to restrict their sodium intake.

1. Spray the pan thoroughly and arrange the fillets that have been patted dry with paper towels.

2. Brush with olive oil, then top with thin slices of onion and thick slices of tomato.

3. Sprinkle herbs on top and put the pan on the grill, closing the top.

4. Check often until the fish flakes easily, then remove grill cover completely, poke holes in the pan to allow drainage and a bit of smoke, then remove the fish and serve.

Materials needed:

Grill with lid
Disposable aluminum pan
Nonstick cooking oil spray
8 to 10 fillets
Olive oil
1 white onion
2 fresh tomatoes
(or more, depending on size)
Fresh thyme or basil

* Select low-calorie, low-salt side dishes for a healthy, tasty meal.

OVEN COOKING

Whether gas or electric, your oven can produce some tasty fish dishes, most of which will fit nicely into a low-calorie, low-cholesterol lifestyle. As already mentioned, many if not most of the recipes given for grilling can be prepared using the stove, and oven cooking provides a lot of other options that the grill just cannot do.

You will find that a number of the recipes which follow can actually be substituted for fried dishes, giving you a wonderfully crunchy outside while keeping oils and fats to a minimum.

Some others may not seem to fit into the mainstream of fish cooking, but don't let that keep you from giving it a try. If all cooks had been squeamish, none of us would have ever tried crawfish, squid, escargot, oysters or many other dishes that fall outside the realm of the common.

Oven Cooking Tips

1. Some dishes such as the foil-wrapped ones allow the fish to sit in various liquids and soak up flavors during cooking while those that are broiled sit under direct heat. When preparing some of the sauce-based recipes, try opening the foil when the dish is cooked, poking holes in the bottom of the foil pan so that the liquid runs into a broiler pan bottom, then turning the oven to the "broil" setting for a couple of minutes. This really perks up the color of the dish, adding a nice brown touch to an otherwise white dish.

2. Remember that every time that you open your oven door you allow the heat to drop dramatically. Keep the door closed unless you are grilling or broiling, and when cooking this way be sure and keep some sort of basting material handy. Plain old olive oil or lemon butter will add moisture and keep the original spices lively.

Catfish Almandine

This recipe came from a formal dinner at a snooty restaurant. I was forced into the situation at a writer's conference and the host of the meal insisted that since I wrote about fishing, I should try the specialty of the house: Trout Almandine. Fortunately the bread, salad and wine were good (not necessarily in that order) so I survived. I find that trout are just not all that great no matter how well you dress them up.

1. Place the fillets in the baking dish and sprinkle with lemon juice, then dust on salt, pepper, paprika and rosemary.

2. Bake for 20 minutes in a 400-degree oven.

3. Sauté the almonds in butter or olive oil until light golden brown.

4. Pour the almonds over the cooked fillets and serve.

Materials needed:

Enough fillets to fill a large greased baking dish
Fresh lemons
1 tablespoon paprika
1/2 teaspoon rosemary
1/4 cup butter or olive oil
1/2 cup sliced or slivered almonds
Salt & pepper to taste

More Fancy Fillets

While on the subject of pretty fishes from the oven, let's look at one more. Although I have not one drop of Italian blood in my veins, I have always loved garlic and various cheeses and this recipe lets me use them in a very tasty way.

1. Rub lemon on catfish the fillets. Dredge the fillets in the butter or oil and pour the remainder into the baking dish.

2. Baste both sides of the fillets with the Catalina dressing, then dip them into the combined spices and bread crumbs.

3. Place the fillets in a single layer, sprinkle on the cheese to suit your own tastes.

4. Bake at 400 degrees for 20 minutes. Adjust baking time to handle thin or thick fillets, but the fish are done when they flake easily with a fork.

Materials needed:

Enough fillets to fill your baking
   dish. Mine is 10 inches by 14
   inches and holds enough for four
   normal people or two fishermen.
1/2 cup melted butter,
   margarine or olive oil
1/2 cup Catalina dressing
1/2 to 1 teaspoon garlic salt
Pepper to taste
1 large lemon
Hungarian paprika
1 cup bread crumbs
   or crushed croutons
Shaker of Parmesan cheese

*
   The same side dishes and beverages
   mentioned earlier are appropriate here.

Namazu

The Japanese home islands, located in the Pacific's volcanic "Ring of Fire," are subject to frequent earthquakes, both large and small. Residents of Edo and other large cities associate earthquakes with the movement of a giant Namazu, or catfish, that lives in the waters deep within the earth. This playful giant catfish causes earthquakes whenever it wiggles or moves.

The movement of the enormous fish would certainly destroy Japan but for a magic boulder and the efforts of a protective deity—the Kashima god. To the northeast of Tokyo on Honshu's Pacific coast is the Kashima Shrine. Buried on the grounds of the shrine is kaname-ishi, or "rivet stone," a great boulder that, tradition says, helps to hold the world together.

In Japanese tradition this huge stone acts as a spiritual safeguard that helps to keep malevolent forces of nature in check. One of its most important functions was to pin down the head of the giant Namazu to keep the creature quiet and immobile. But the weight of the kaname-ishi alone cannot keep the catfish quiet. The Kashima god must lend a hand by pushing down on the stone. At times, however, the deity's mind wanders or he falls asleep allowing the Namazu to thrash about, which results in an earthquake. The Kashima god then has to struggle to regain control.

Steamed & Superb

Another great way to fix dishes without the benefit of oils or grease is to do it in the oven. Since you will be cooking with steam here, the process could actually be called poaching, but that word has such a negative connotation that I am reluctant to use it.

1. Spray the broiler pan rack with nonstick cooking oil spray. Fill the pan about 1/4 full of water. I generally add the peel of the onion being used, a tablespoon of salt and of pepper, and some oregano to the water just for the sake of aroma.

2. Set the pan with the water on top of the stove over high heat until it begins to boil.

3. Put the rack on the pan, then lay on the fish, separated for even cooking. Baste liberally with melted margarine or butter.

4. Grind a half-cup of bell pepper and another of onion. Combine the two and add the juice of 1 lemon. Mix, then spread on top of your steaks, fillets or small whole fish.

5. Sprinkle with salt, pepper and oregano. Cover with heavy-duty aluminum foil and crimp it tightly in place around the edges.

6. Place in a 375-degree oven for 15 minutes for average fillets, 20 minutes for small whole fish, and

Materials needed:

2 pounds of catfish
Broiler pan
Aluminum foil
Nonstick cooking oil spray
White onion
Bell pepper
Lemon
Salt & pepper
Oregano
Margarine or butter, melted

30 minutes for larger ones.

7. Remove from the oven, then split and remove the foil, being careful to avoid scalding from the steam.

8. Flip the oven to Broil, return the fish to the oven and watch them closely. When they are nicely browned around the edges, remove and serve.

* A nice cheese sauce makes an interesting topping, but the fish are ready to eat as they come from the stove.

Not His Favorite Fish

This singular and hideous family of fishes is distinguished
from the others of the same order, by the skin being either
naked or protected by large plates, but always destitute
of true scales... This family contains twenty-five or
thirty species peculiar to America, which are generally
known as Cat-fish, Bull-heads, Bull-pouts, &c...

The commonest and the largest species both belong to the
subgenus Pimelodeus, and are well known as Cat-fish; the
ordinary kind measuring only a few inches in length, and
never exceeding a few ounces in weight; the largest reaching
a hundred or even a hundred and fifty pounds, especially in
the great northern lakes, and in the western rivers...

The skin is smooth, thick, adipose, and lubricated by a
mucous secretion. The color is a dingy greenish brown
above, and dirty white below. The flesh is very rich and
gelatinous, and not dissimilar either in quality or flavor to
that of the eel... All the Cat-fish are greedy biters, and
will take almost any animal substance as bait. After being
hooked, however, although they are powerful fish, and pull
hard for a while, it is yet a dead lug entirely, unlike the
lively and fierce resistance of the Trouts and Pearches;
and they afford in truth very little sport to the angler.

Frank Forester's Fish and Fishing of the United States
—William Herbert, 1851

Crunchy Chip Fish

I mentioned that it is possible to get a crispy, tasty product out of the oven, and here is one way to get just that result. It is so idiot-proof that even the worst, least ingenious cook can come out looking good with this offering. For those who are trying to get their young-sters to eat healthy, here is a starting point. There is no way that you can convince them that potato chips do not automatically equate to junk food.

1. Crush the chips and add any spices. Reduce them to very small particles for even coverage of the breading. Place in a shaking bag.

2. Drop the damp fillets in and shake well to coat.

3. Place the fillets so that they do not touch on a nonstick baking sheet and bake at 325 degrees until brown. See how easy that is?

Materials needed:

Baking sheet or other large, flat pan
2 pounds of fillets in water
Package of potato chips
 (Get low-fat, low-sodium if you like. I use Pringel's because they hold less oil and are very easy to crush into a breading material.)
Salt & pepper if desired
Dash of oregano or paprika

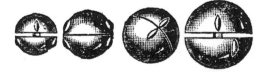

Hurry-Up Micro Fillets

There are numerous ways to cook catfish in your microwave, so don't be afraid to experiment. Here is an easy one that will help you get started.

1. Mix the spices together and whip into the melted butter.

2. Pour enough of the mixture into the pie plate to cover the bottom; arrange fillets tightly, and then pour in the rest of the butter and spice mixture.

3. Cover with plastic wrap and prick a small hole for steam to escape.

4. Cook on High for 3 ½ to 4 minutes or until the fillets in the middle flake easily.

Materials needed:

Enough small fillets
   to fill a 9-inch pie plate
   (not metal)
1/4 cup melted butter
Juice from 1/2 a lemon
Dash of garlic powder
Dash of onion powder
Salt & pepper to taste

* This quick-and-easy dish with minimal cleanup was at least moderately famous during the period when my daughter lived in a college dorm and prepared it frequently in the communal kitchen. Its popularity faded when the students found out that their fillet supply ended upon Libby's graduation.

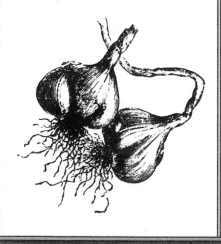

Another Pizza Fish Recipe

Since we are keeping things simple, here is another dish that can be prepared very easily. Because the spices give off an aroma like a pizza joint, it is also another option for kids who have the culinary aspirations and appreciation of a doorknob.

1. Pat the fillets dry with paper towels, then sprinkle with lemon juice.

2. Place them on the baking pan and dust lightly with the oregano or Italian seasoning.

3. Spread the pasta sauce over each piece of fish and sprinkle on the cheese.

4. Bake in a hot oven (450 to 500 degrees) for about 15 minutes or until the fish flakes easily.

Materials needed:

Shallow, nonstick baking pan
2 to 3 pounds of fillets
1 lemon
1 teaspoon oregano or
    prepared dry Italian seasoning
1 jar prepared pasta sauce
    (Prego, Ragu, etc.)
1 package shredded mozzarella
    cheese. (You can also use
    Parmesan cheese which almost
    all of us have around the house.)

* Since kids may shy away from their veggies, at least have some garlic breadsticks to go with this dish. If they don't eat them they can at least pretend to be fencing with them or using them for walrus tusks when your back is turned.

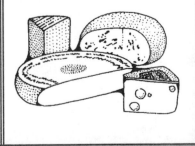

Finest Eatin'

"Catfish? Who sesso? Hit's the bes' eatin' fish you kin git anywhere. Don't keer where you go. There aint nothin' that tickle your palate like a chunk of channel cat fried crisp. Of co'se de snot cat good. Th' ole mud cat aint bad neither. I have eat pompano and buffalo fish and red snapper and a lot of others. But don't let nobody tell you any different. Catfish is the finest eatin of all."

—George Sims, 1939, in "The Black South in Chicago," WPA L. C. Project Writers' Unit, Folklore Collection

Pat's "Cumbersome" Preference

My wife and I have been together since sometime between the Battle of Gettysburg and Lee's surrender at Appomattox, or so she says. On many things we agree, but this recipe is not one of them. I believe that cucumbers are made to be converted into pickles, not cooked or served raw. As a youngster on the farm, I often tried to get livestock such as cows and pigs to eat the elongated, warty vegetables but they refused. I hope to be at least as smart as a pig despite the fact that restaurants, and apparently some people, think that they are edible—cucumbers, not pigs. To paraphrase a popular advertising line, "Dear, this dud's for you."

1. Just to be safe, hit the inside of your cooking pan with one of the nonstick cooking oil sprays.

2. Allow most of the water to drip from the fillets, then place them in a single layer in the pan.

3. Combine all the other ingredients and smear it over the poor fillets.

4. Broil for 5 to 6 minutes. The top will be brown, making the whole affair look not only edible, but tasty. Blame it on Pat.

Materials needed:

Nonstick baking sheet or
   other shallow pan
2 pounds of fillets
   (small ones preferred)
1/2 cup chopped (yuk) cucumber
1/4 cup finely chopped onion
Juice from 1/2 lemon
1 teaspoon soy sauce
1/2 cup mayonnaise
   (not salad dressing)
Salt & pepper to taste

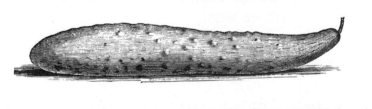

Can He Drive, Too?

One day a boy and his uncle went down at the river to do some catfishing. They had been out for a while when the uncle felt a steady pull on the line. "Boy," he said, "I'm pretty sure I've hooked a nice big cat down there." He began to reel the fish in, but it just pulled harder and harder. Try as he might he couldn't haul that fish up off the bottom. "I know I ain't hooked no snag," the old man said, "I can feel it moving!"

He pulled and heaved, and he heaved and pulled, but he couldn't drag that fish up to the boat. After a while the fish quit moving and just sat there. "I guess the line's caught up on something," he said turning to his nephew. "Son, here's what I want you to do. You're a good swimmer. You jump in and follow that line down and find out where it's caught at, knock it loose and we'll have that catfish for sure."

The boy shucked off his shoes and slid over the side of the boat and disappeared into the brown water. After a few moments he popped to the surface sputtering. "Uncle, you're going to have to cut the line!" he shouted.

The old fisherman looked puzzled. "Why should I to do that?"

"Well," said the boy, "Down about ten feet you've got about a fifty pound cat on the hook and he's holed-up in the back seat of the old Ford that Bill Jones run in here last year."

"You just swim back down there and give him a good poke, he'll come out and we'll have him."

"I already tried that," said the boy, "but he rolled the window up on me!"

Sweet Fillets à la Center Hill

Another friend who has gone to the Great Fishing Hole In The Sky was a fisheries biologist by the name of Jim Little. Jim was the first person ever to swear to me that woodcock were not only edible, but good. I always suspected that he had impaired taste buds.

Jim also produced one of the darndest fish recipes that I have yet unearthed in more than thirty years of searching. We were sharing a houseboat on Center Hill Lake when he slipped this one in and it took me a long time to forgive him. Of course, since I really do not even care for jelly on toast, the fault on this one could be mine. In any event, I hope that you will try it. Should you find it tasty, please write my publisher or me and let us know. If you agree with me that sweets have no place in fish cooking, tell Jim.

1. Spray the pan with the non-stick vegetable cooking spray and lay the fillets inside after patting them dry with paper towels and dipping them into a mixture of all the other ingredients, which should be well blended.

2. Arrange the orange slices atop each fillet and bake for 12 to 15 minutes, until flaky, at 350 degrees.

Materials needed:

Medium-sized baking pan
2 pounds of catfish fillets
1 stick butter or margarine
1 orange, peeled, sliced with seeds
    removed
1 jar orange marmalade
1/4 cup honey
Nonstick vegetable cooking spray

*
   This is a pretty dish, one that looks wonderful when accompanied by a green salad, yellow corn, heck, anything with color. I just wish that I liked it.

Really Big Fish

The United States is home to the "big three" of North American catfish—blue, flathead and channel—which rank among the world's largest. In August 2001 Charles Ashley Jr. was fishing for catfish on the Arkansas side of the Mississippi River near West Memphis when he reeled in a 116-pound, 12-ounce blue cat—a probable world record. Ashley used a chunk of Spam for bait. A world-record flathead catfish, which tipped the scales at 123 pounds 9 ounces, was caught by Ken Paulie in 1999 in the Elk City Reservoir, Kansas. The record blue catfish, weighing 111 pounds was caught by William McKinley in Wheeler's Reservoir, Tennessee, on July 5, 1996.

More Peppers & Fish

Having purchased a number of mild peppers for a different dish, my friend, "The Sloan," came up with another use for them. This recipe began as an afterthought but soon became one of our favorites, especially for cooking in the oven. He also served a side dish that I feel compelled to share. It follows the main course here.

1. Put a dash of cooking oil and another of vinegar into the food processor, then dump in the garlic powder, salt and pepper.

2. Purée and let it sit in the refrigerator for 30 minutes.

3. Place the fillets on the nonstick pan, sprinkle the chopped peppers and onion liberally on the fish and top with the refrigerated purée mixture.

4. Depending on the thickness of the fillets, broil for 10 to 12 minutes. The tops should be nice and brown while the flesh flakes easily.

Materials needed:

Shallow nonstick pan
Food processor
2 pounds of fillets
Cooking oil
Salt & pepper to taste
1/2 teaspoon garlic powder
Vinegar
1/2 cup diced green pepper
1/2 cup diced red pepper
(You can actually use 1 cup of any kind of sweet pepper rather than 1/2 cup of each.)
1/2 cup chopped white onion

Now for the side dish:

1. Take 2 large yellow onions and 2 (minimum) large bell peppers. Slice all into 1/4- to 1/2-inch strips. 2. Place the onions first into a large skillet with a lid that fits, add the juice of 2 lemons, no seeds please, 2 tablespoons of Worcestershire sauce and cook for 5 minutes over medium heat. 3. Remove the lid, add the peppers and cook for another 5 minutes. 4. Serve with a dash of soy sauce. I promise that you will be surprised at the result.

Whiskerfish Wontons

This recipe was passed along by a friend who is an unabashed walleye fishing nut. He remains this way despite the fact that I have repeatedly pointed out that if one tied a walleye and catfish of equal size tail to tail, my fish would pull his around all day and hardly notice the load. Since he refuses to admit to the obvious, I stole his recipe.

1. Into a large skillet or sauté pan pour about one-half cup olive oil and heat until it smokes slightly.

2. Add the catfish, celery and carrots and cook for 2 minutes before adding the bell pepper and onions and sautéing for 2 more minutes.

3. Add the mushrooms and leave on the heat for about a minute more.

4. Add the wine and stir frequently until the wine is absorbed completely, then set the mixture aside in a mixing bowl to cool.

5. Mix in the bread crumbs, egg whites and tarragon.

6. Run through a meat grinder or food processor on low setting.

7. Wrap small portions of the mixture in wonton wrappers, then deep fry at 330 to 350 degrees in the oil until golden brown.

Materials needed:

Virgin olive oil
1 pound chopped fillets
1 cup diced celery
1 cup diced carrots
1 cup chopped bell pepper
1 1/2 cups chopped onions
1 cup chopped mushrooms
1 cup full-bodied red wine
1 cup bread crumbs
2 egg whites
Dash of tarragon
12 wonton wrappers
Salt & pepper to taste

*

Anticipate a ready reception for this finger food for kids and grownups alike. Whiskerfish wontons are super snacks when you are waiting for more serious dishes to come to the table.

Lemon-Dill Dandies

Here is another easy recipe that I like very much. Except for the butter, it is also great for those on a serious diet, and what the heck, everybody has to splurge a little now and then. If you are the serious type, substitute margarine even though the final product will not be quite as tasty.

1. Dry the fillets, rub with lemon then put them on a nonstick baking pan or baking sheet.

2. Combine the butter, wine and any seasonings except for salt and pepper, then pour it over the fillets.

3. I grow my own dill, so it is no problem to shred some to sprinkle over the top; but if you do not have an herb garden (and you should, they're fun), use the dry stuff found in the seasoning section at the supermarket.

4. Lightly dust each fillet, then follow with salt and pepper.

5. Place under the broiler until the fish flakes easily.

Materials needed:

Shallow baking pan
  (baking sheet, etc.; nonstick type)
2 pounds of fillets
Juice from 2 lemons
1/4 cup white wine,
  Chenin Blanc works well
2 sticks butter, melted
Dill, or dillweed
  as it is sometimes known
Salt & pepper to taste

* If you have a favorite spice, try it here. I have used everything from ground cayenne pepper to oregano to curry powder.

Catfish Walkin'

The walking catfish (clarias batrachus) has an air-breathing organ made of modified gill filaments and can walk over land on rainy nights, using the tips of its stout pectoral spines as pivots as it shoves itself along by flexing its body. This Asian native, introduced into Florida waters in the late 1960s, is abundant in southern and central parts of the state. When asked if he had heard of walking catfish, one wag quipped, "Yeah, I picked up a bunch of them on the road the other night ... they were hitchhiking to West Virginia!"

102# Blue Cat

Game Fish Elegante

Here is another easy dish, but one which will have dinner guests thinking two things: (1) you have more money than they imagined, and (2) you went to a lot of trouble in order to impress them. It is a great one to spring on obnoxious in-laws or old school chums who have since made it big in advertising, real estate, used cars, politics, the legal profession or any similar questionable field. I will never tell them the truth but just to keep things even between us, you really should go out and buy another copy of this book.

1. Use a shallow baking dish (you can also prepare this one on the grill; I just never think of it until the holidays when the weather is lousy).

2. Open the crabmeat or shrimp and save the liquid.

3. Mix it with enough seasoned bread crumbs to make a heavy dough, then put the crabmeat or shrimp into the dough.

4. Layer it over the fillets. Salt and pepper to taste.

5. Mix the melted butter, lemon juice and soy sauce and add it gently on top, being careful not to wash away the coating.

6. Cook at 350 degrees until the meat flakes easily (20 to 30 minutes). Thick fillets may take longer. Some cooks add a dash of paprika, and I even know one who uses a dash of ground sage. Seeing no sense in gilding the lily, I serve it as is.

Materials needed:

2 pounds of fillets
1-pound can crabmeat
   or miniature shrimp
1 box seasoned bread crumbs
Salt & pepper
1 stick butter, melted
Juice from 2 lemons
Dash of soy sauce

*You can prepare your choice of vegetable side dishes but if anything more than a salad is really needed, that fact has escaped my guests and me. Now and then, sneak some cherrystone clams into the mix for fun.

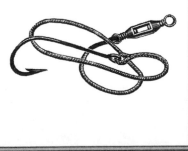

"Noodling" Indian Style

James Adair, an Indian trader and historian, lived among the Chickasaws and Cherokees during the early 18th century. In his book History of the Indian Nations, published in 1775, Adair described "a surprising method of fishing under the edges of rocks" among the southern Indians:

"They pull off their red breeches, or their long slip of Stroud cloth, and wrapping it round their arm, so as to reach to the lower part of the palm of their right hand, they dive under the rock where the cat-fish lie to shelter themselves from the scorching beams of the sun, and to watch for prey: as soon as those fierce aquatic animals see that tempting bait, they immediately seize it with the greatest violence, in order to swallow it. Then is the time for the diver to improve the favourable opportunity: he accordingly opens his hand, seizes the voracious fish by his tender parts, hath a sharp struggle with it against the crevices of the rock, and at last brings it safe ashore."

History of the Indian Nations
—James Adair, 1775

Classic Casserole

When it comes to simplicity, a casserole dish has a lot going for it. With the easier ones you just dump some good tasting ingredients together and wait for the heat of the oven to work its magic. This one is almost that easy, and it is awfully good.

1. This is a multi-step recipe, but not a tough one. Put the fillets in the dish along with the tomato sauce and spices and cook for about 20 minutes or until the fish flakes easily.

2. While they are cooking, mix the cream cheese, chopped onions and sour cream and set it aside.

3. Cook the egg noodles or potatoes.

4. Melt butter in the dish. When all is ready, put the noodles or potatoes in the bottom of the casserole dish, cooked fish atop that, then the cream cheese mixture. Keep doing this brick-laying method until you run out of materials and then add a layer of your favorite cheese on top.

5. Bake for 30 minutes at low heat, 250 to 275 degrees.

6. Upon removing the casserole from the oven you may wish to add a thin layer of seasoned bread crumbs to the top.

Materials needed:

Large casserole dish
  (you really need 2)
2 to 3 pounds of fillets
1/2 cup chopped onions
1-pound bag of egg noodles or
  2 cups cooked, stewed potatoes
8-ounce package cream cheese,
  well softened
1 stick butter, melted
1 cup sour cream
Cheese: cheddar, mozzarella or
  Monterey Jack
1 teaspoon garlic powder
Salt & pepper to taste
16-ounce can tomato sauce

* I once got daring and added thinly sliced pepperoni to the bubbly cheese top. My guests picked off the pepperoni, so I leave such touches to your discretion.

"Generally Well Supplied With Catfish"

For Lewis and Clark's Corps of Discovery, fish were both objects of study and a source of provisions. Meriweather Lewis ordered fishing equipment for his expedition from George Lawson's "Old Experienced Tackle Shop" in Philadelphia. At a cost of $25.37, Lewis purchased 125 hooks, several dozen assorted fishing lines, and an 8 stave reel. He also bought lines and hooks as gifts for Indians. Various members of the expedition recorded encounters with the Missouri River's white catfish:

"...as we came along Shore there was two large Cat fish had hold of Each other could not get off one of the french men Shot the two the first Shot."
—Joseph Whitehouse, July 19, 1804

"Set out at 5 o'clock opposite the island—the bend to the right or S.S. within 20 feet of Indian Knob Creek. The water of this creek is 5 feet higher than that of the river. Past the island we stopped to dine under some high trees near the high land on the L.S. In a few minutes, caught three very large catfish, one nearly white. Those fish are in great plenty on the sides of the river and very fat. A quart of oil came out of the surplus fat of one of those fish."
—Captain Clark, White Catfish Camp, July 26, 1804

"We are generally well supplied with Catfish, the best I have ever seen. Some large ones were taken last night."
—Patrick Gass, August 29, 1804

Garden Catfish Casserole

Here's one that is easy to put together after you've spent a morning in the garden harvesting fresh veggies. You can buy them of course but I'm addicted to the specimens from my backyard. Although the original recipe calls for butter and cheese, you can substitute olive oil or use low-fat substitutes and have a heart-smart dish that can be prepared ahead of time and kept in the refrigerator.

1. While your oven is preheating to 450 degrees, arrange the vegetables and fillets in layers. Repeat until all of the ingredients are used.

2. On each of the fillets, brush on olive oil or place a pat of butter, then sprinkle with spices.

3. Cover the dish and bake for 45 minutes to 1 hour, depending on the thickness of the fillets.

4. Remove the dish from the oven, remove the cover and sprinkle liberally with cheese and an additional dusting of paprika.

5. Put the dish back in the oven without the lid and bake for another 10 to 15 minutes.

6. Check the vegetables with a toothpick or skewer and when the carrots are tender, you're ready to eat.

Materials needed:

Casserole dish or baking pan
6 to 8 fillets
3 or 4 potatoes,
   sliced about 1/2 inch thick
3 or 4 carrots, sliced
1 large onion, sliced
2 tablespoons dill weed
1 teaspoon rosemary
Paprika, salt and pepper to taste
Butter or olive oil
1 cup grated or shredded
   Parmesan cheese

Simply Delicious Baked Fillets

Like most people who enjoy cooking, I have favorites in the spice department, brands that have delivered consistent, reliable quality over a lengthy period of time. One such company sells under the Lawry name and although there may be other products similar to the one mentioned here, I have never found anything as good and certainly nothing better.

1. Put the fillets in a plastic freezer bag, add the Lawry's marinade and let sit for at least 2 hours.

2. Remove and pat dry, then roll in crushed seasoned bread crumbs.

3. Arrange in a baking dish that has been buttered or sprayed with nonstick vegetable spray and sprinkle liberally with lemon pepper. Sprinkle on salt.

4. Combine the sour cream, mayonnaise and onions and spread over the fillets.

5. Sprinkle with paprika and bake at 500 degrees for 15 to 20 minutes until the surface is light brown and bubbling freely.

Materials needed:

2 pounds of fillets
(1) 12-ounce bottle Lawry's
    Mesquite Marinade
    with Lemon Juice
3/4 cup real mayonnaise
1½ cups sour cream
3/4 cup finely chopped onions
Seasoned bread crumbs
Salt & lemon pepper to taste
Dash of Hungarian paprika

Break convention when serving. Try serving with a baked potato and corn on the cob with some hot, crusty rolls to complement things.

*This is an easy main dish to fix and mighty tasty. It is also part of a healthy eating regimen for those who concern themselves with such things.

Cheesy Catfish

Break out your casserole or baking dish again and put the spice rack where you can reach it. No cook can combine three kinds of cheese with anything and not want to add a little something extra. I usually sprinkle on some Italian variation, but here is the basic formula. You can provide the fine touches.

1. Oil a baking pan and lay the fillets in place.

2. Sprinkle with the spices, then cover with the soup.

3. Add the cheddar cheese followed by the mozzarella and bake at 350 degrees for 25 minutes or longer, depending on the thickness of the fillets. Check to see when they flake easily with a fork.

4. Remove the pan from the oven and add the Parmesan cheese, then put it back into the oven and bake for 15 minutes or until the cheese starts to bubble and brown.

Materials needed:

Enough fillets to fill the dish
    without overlapping
1 can cream of celery soup
Salt & pepper to taste
Dash of Hungarian paprika
Equal amounts of grated
    or shredded mozzarella and
    cheddar cheese (sufficient to
    cover the fillets)
Shaker of grated Parmesan
    or bag of shredded cheese

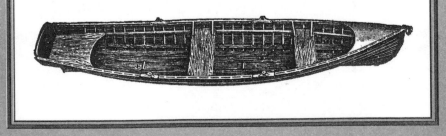

Pepper Jack Fillets

Regardless of the type of main dish being prepared, I often look for an excuse to use cheese of some kind. One or more of my ex-wives have hinted that this may be due to some sort of rodent ancestry but I don't care; cheese is good and this recipe lets me combine some dairy products with catfish fillets. It is a tasty combination anytime and is perfect for a chilly, nasty winter day when both you and your taste buds need something to brighten things up.

1. Make an aluminum foil boat to fit a large baking sheet or baking pan and coat it liberally with a nonstick oil spray, preferably olive oil or canola oil.

2. Put the fillets in the boat and sprinkle with the seasoned salt and lemon pepper and place in a preheated 400-degree oven for 15 minutes.

3. Remove the pan from the oven and add the peppers, onion and cheese, then return to the oven for at least 5 minutes.

4. When the cheese is thoroughly melted, the meal is ready but you may prefer to wait until the part around the edges starts to brown.

Materials needed:

6 to 8 catfish fillets
1 medium red onion, chopped
1 small can chopped green chilies
    (You can substitute fresh stuff,
    even jalapeños if you like.)
1/2 pound shredded
    cheddar cheese
1/2 pound shredded
    Pepper Jack cheese
Seasoned salt and
    lemon pepper to taste

*This is a beer-and-buddies dish that you might want to consider the next time that the weather keeps you inside and there is a good ball game on the tube. Use corn chips to dip the remaining cheese and fillet fragments from the foil boat.

Continental Casserole

I brought this recipe home after an extended working trip a few years back. The journey had covered three western states and a bit of Canada, and a lot of time was spent in camp talking about (and eating) food. You can't climb mountains living on clean air and high country water, so we ate and ate well. The recipe survived, but the person who provided it has unfortunately been mis-remembered. Maybe he or she will buy a copy of this cookbook and give me a call.

1. Spray the casserole dish with the nonstick vegetable oil and place the fillets in it.

2. Mix 2 to 3 tablespoons of cooking oil with salt, pepper and oregano or Italian seasoning and allow it to sit while you get the rest of the act together.

3. Combine all the other ingredients in a pan and cook until the onions are soft, which will be about 10 minutes.

4. Pour the mixture over the fish, sprinkle on the bread crumbs and bake at 375 degrees for about 30 minutes or longer if the fillets are thick.

* This is the basis of a great meal. I just wish that I could remember who wrote it in pencil on a piece of an instant mashed potato box.

Materials needed:

Casserole dish
Nonstick vegetable spray
2 pounds of fillets
Cooking oil
2 cups peeled and diced tomatoes
(canned will work)
1/2 cup finely chopped onion
1 teaspoon garlic powder
Juice from 1 lemon
2 teaspoons oregano
or dry Italian seasoning
1 cup commercial seasoned bread
crumbs
Chopped, dried parsley
1/2 cup Chablis or Sauterne
(back in the booze again)
Salt & pepper to taste

There's a Really Big Fish Down There!

The story usually goes something like this: "I'll tell you the truth there are some really BIG catfish in this (lake, river)! Why I was talking to (a friend of mine, the local game warden, the sheriff) and he told me that a while back they sent some divers down to (repair the bridge, find a body, examine the base of the dam). After a few minutes the diver came up looking pale. He said that when he reached the bottom he came face-to-face with a catfish that was as big as (a cow, a sofa, a piano, an SUV). That diver was so scared he wouldn't go back down again!"

There is sometimes a second part to the story. In the case of lakes with hydroelectric dams, the argument goes, the dam's turbines take in all sorts of nutrients along with the water flow, such as small fish, etc. and expel the chopped-up remains through the outlet pipes at the base of the dam. This "nutrient sink" attracts catfish and, since it is assumed that there is no biological limit to a catfish's size, the fish keep on growing. Stories abound of anglers hooking giant catfish that they could not land, but no one has yet caught one of these sofa-sized giants. Most biologists argue that such tales are apocryphal.

Once upon a time, however, monster cats did indeed inhabit Southern waters. In 1983, a geologist working in the vicinity of Camden, Arkansas, found a fragment of fossil bone protruding from a dirt embankment. Attached was a two-foot-long skull. The beast was determined to be a 10-foot-long, 1,500-pound catfish that prowled Arkansas' Eocene waters about 40 million years ago.

Art's Casserole

This one is easy to remember. It came from my buddy Art Davies. At last count we have been in four countries together, doing the things that we do, and traveling with Art means eating well. He knows and appreciates food, and he can jolly well cook. This recipe was tested on a redfish outing off the Cajun Coast and proved perfectly applicable to catfish and other species. If you think that everything prepared in Louisiana is meant to test your pepper tolerance, this will be a pleasant surprise. It was for me.

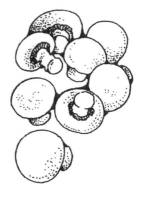

1. If using the bell pepper, sauté it and the onion in butter until soft.

2. Hold the pimento pepper for later if you elect to use the olive-stuffers.

3. Blend in the mayonnaise and mushroom soup and add salt and pepper to taste.

4. Place the fillets in the casserole dish and ladle the sauce on top, then add the mozzarella cheese and pimento if you are going that route.

5. Bake at 350 degrees for 30 minutes or longer if using thick fillets. Once the fish flakes easily in the middle of the dish, it is done.

Materials needed:

Casserole dish
2 pounds of fillets
1 white onion, chopped
  (tennis ball size)
1 can Campbell's cream of
  mushroom soup
1/4 cup chopped pimento or
1/4 cup finely chopped bell pepper
1/4 cup mayonnaise
1/4 cup grated mozzarella cheese
2 tablespoons butter
Salt & pepper

* Art says to serve it over dirty rice, but plain old "clean" white rice will work. It is also good over wild rice or even in the company of someone named Rice.

Almost a Casserole

Here is another one of those simple yet tasty dishes that makes putting a whole meal together a snap. If you find out at the last minute that unexpected guests are coming, whip up a simple salad, open a can of peas or beans, maybe one of corn unless you have some "on the cob" variety in the freezer, and try this dish as the center of the main course. Once again, you can save the wine not used for cooking and serve it later.

1. Place the fillets in a nonstick dish, thanks to the vegetable spray; salt and pepper them and then pour the rest of the ingredients over the top.

2. Cook uncovered at 375 degrees for 30 to 45 minutes until the fish flakes easily.

Materials needed:

Glass baking dish (metal will work)
2 pounds of catfish fillets
Nonstick vegetable spray
Juice from 1/2 lemon
1 cup white wine
   (Chablis or Sauterne)
1 cup tomato sauce or
   1 ½ cups canned tomatoes
Salt & pepper
Oregano (optional)
Prepared Parmesan cheese
   (optional)

Another Easy Option

Just as with the previous recipe, this is about as simple as it gets. You just wind up with a different taste.

1. Squirt the fillets with lemon juice, then salt and pepper.

2. Place the fillets in a casserole dish sprayed with nonstick vegetable spray, then add the sour cream, grated onion, horseradish and cheese and sprinkle with the seasoned bread crumbs.

3. Bake at 350 degrees for about 45 minutes, depending on the thickness of the fillets.

Materials needed:

Casserole dish
2 pounds of fillets
Nonstick vegetable spray
Seasoned bread crumbs
1/4 cup grated onion
1/3 cup sour cream
4 tablespoons prepared horseradish
Parmesan cheese
    (grated mozzarella will work)
Salt & pepper to taste
Juice from 1 lemon

Bucket Fishing

In Louisiana, catfishermen sometimes employ an
unusual cat-catching technique called bucket fishing.
The participants submerge weighted buckets with a
semicircular hole cut in the lid. Catfish enter the
containers to spawn and are captured by lifting the
containers from the water using an attached line.

Caught out of
Ark. River
1911

Broiled Spicy Fish

If this recipe has a drawback, it is simply that it must be considered seasonal. Fresh peppers, preferably straight from the garden are virtually essential to get the most from this one. Like the Mexi-Chunk Fish recipe, it is also one that can run from bland to burning.

1. Place aluminum foil over the grill rack and perforate it well. Spray it with nonstick vegetable spray.

2. Drain the fish on paper towels and place on rack. Rub with lemon. Fillets work best here although whole fish can be used. Dust fish with salt, pepper and garlic powder.

3. On each piece, alternate strips of hot pepper, bell pepper and onion. For extra zing, run a second row of peppers at right angles with the first.

4. Baste the combination with olive oil and place over your heat source and cover.

5. For cooking times, use those given in the other grilled fish recipes.

Materials needed:

2 pounds of catfish
Fresh hot peppers
  (Cayenne, both young and
  mature preferred although
  jalapeño, Thai or others will
  suffice. Stay away from habanero
  because of its strong taste.)
Bell pepper
Purple onion
Lemon
Salt & pepper
Garlic salt or powder
Aluminum foil
Nonstick vegetable spray
Olive oil

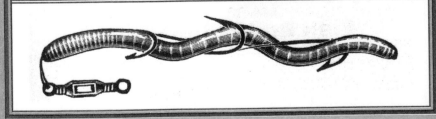

Smoked Fish

Given the number of solutions in which fish can be immersed prior to smoking, this short segment of the book could in fact be made into a book of its own. We are going to stick with brevity here simply because this is an area that literally begs for experimentation on the part of the cook. These recipes are also intended for use on lean specimens such as walleye, bass and catfish, but will work on just about anything.

1. Bring the whole affair to a boil, then reduce the heat and allow it to simmer for 10 minutes.

2. Remove from heat, pour into a glass or plastic container and allow it to cool in the refrigerator.

3. When cool, add as many small fish or fillets as the liquid will adequately cover. Refrigerate overnight.

4. After at least 8 hours, remove, drain and wash with cold water. Place on racks to dry. An electric fan works well here. The fish should not go into the smoker until they are dry. If wet, they tend to get dark and may become too strong in flavor due to the smoke "sticking" to them.

5. Once dry, place the fish in a dry, low-heat smoker.

6. Over a 6- to 8-hour period, use two pans of apple, alder or hickory wood chips. The fish should still be moist, but will flake easily and have a gentle smoky taste.

Materials needed:

Basic Brine Solution
While it is certainly possible to smoke fish without the prior use of a brine solution, the flavor will not be much. I know—I've tried it. Try this for a marinade and you should produce a winner no matter what you decide to add.

10 cups water
1 cup pickling and canning salt
2 bay leaves
1 tablespoon onion powder
1 teaspoon garlic powder
2 tablespoons chili powder
1 teaspoon celery seed

Bear in mind that lean fish are different from the more oily salmonids. Because of their lean nature, they soak up the seasonings in various brine solutions in a marvelous manner.

* Hey, I don't stick my nose up in the air when someone offers me a taste of their smoked carp.

Smoky Cheese/Fish Dip

The first year that I entered cooking competition, I also provided some snacks for visiting members of the press. No one told me that among them was the head of the judging team, so when I saw him using his finger to get the last of the dip out of the bowl, it had no special significance. I was just happy that the recipe, a new one, had gone over well. Two nights later I walked away with a trophy the size of a fire hydrant—the dip had won it even before he tasted my actual entry.

CHEDDAR

1. Start with smoked fish according to the previous recipe's instructions, then for each pound of smoked fish add the ingredients listed.

2. If you like cheese balls, leave out the sour cream, make a ball out of the dip and roll it in crushed walnuts or thinly sliced pecans.

*
My daughter once decided to get fancy and made a cheese and smoked fish turtle with a cauliflower head, stuffed pimento eyes and broccoli legs and tail. That seemed like a lot of work for something that we were going to eat anyway.

Materials needed:

1/2 pound cream cheese
1/4 pound sour cream
1/4 pound mild cheddar
Juice from 1 lemon
1/2 cup finely chopped onions
1 teaspoon of prepared horseradish

On occasion I have also added such things as chives, pimento and chopped Spanish olives.

DIFFERENT & DELICIOUS

Many fish work well in various chowders, stews, gumbos, cakes, pies and various other dishes seldom seen outside specialty restaurants. Here are a few of my favorites including Yumbo Gumbo, another award-winning recipe.

Yumbo Gumbo

This began as a bona fide Cajun recipe from one of New Orleans' top restaurants. As good as it was, I could not leave well enough alone and made a few alterations. The final version is better suited to the use of lean fish than the original.

Also, this recipe does not include the use of a roux, or thickening, made from browned flour and oil. It is a clear-based soup that makes an excellent appetizer with just about any meal, and it is great on its own when cold winter winds make you want something warm and friendly. Incidentally, this is a great recipe which allows you to use those small bluegill and other panfish that frequently need to be removed from overcrowded ponds.

1. Prepare the shrimp and crab boil according to the instructions on the package and drop in the fish. For fillets, cook for 4 minutes, remove from heat and allow to sit for 5 minutes. Whole fish should be cooked at least 5 to 6 minutes, then allowed to sit for 5 minutes.

2. In a skillet, sauté the green pepper, okra, chopped onion and hot peppers in 3 tablespoons of butter until soft.

3. Add these to the consommé, cooked tomatoes and bay leaves.

4. Boil softly for 15 minutes.

5. Add 1 cup of cooked, flaked fish and 1 tablespoon of minced parsley. This is also the time to add any optional ingredients with the possible exception of the cooked rice. Some rice takes on the consistency of library paste if cooked too long.

6. Allow the pot to simmer for 10 minutes or so before serving.

For larger pots of gumbo, multiply the ingredients accordingly. I have put this list together to make enough gumbo to serve four normal people or two fishermen.

* If your family and friends are like mine, their comments after eating will be more than worth the price of this cookbook. That means that you got all the other recipes for free.

Materials needed:

Medium-sized skillet,
  cast iron preferred
4-quart or larger cooker
1 pound fillets or 2-pound whole fish
1 package shrimp & crab boil
  (I use Zatarain's)
1 lemon
1/4 cup chopped green pepper
1 1/2 cups sliced okra
1/4 cup chopped onion
Cayenne or other hot peppers to taste
1 quart consommé
  (Chicken bouillon, 1 cube equals
  1 cup of broth, or you can boil
  some dead creature.)
2 1/2 cups cooked tomatoes
  (*2 can)
Butter
2 bay leaves
1 tablespoon minced parsley
1 cup cooked rice (optional)
1 can whole kernel corn (optional)

Making a Roux

For a more conventional gumbo, add a roux to the gumbo recipe above.

1. To make it, use 1/2 cup flour and 1/2 cup cooking oil.
2. Stir continuously over medium heat until the mixture takes on a rich, hearty brown color with no odor of burning.
3. Stir the roux into the gumbo and let it simmer for a heartier dish.

Cat Eats Dog

In July 2003, several European news sources reported that a gardener had discovered the carcass of "Kuno the Killer" catfish washed up on the shores of a lake in the public gardens near Moenchengladbach, Germany. The 1.5-meter- (5-foot)-long whiskered monster made headlines in 2001 after he reportedly sprang from the water and swallowed a dachshund puppy whole. A few tufts of fur and a collar were all that was ever found of the dog. Despite the canine addition to his menu, wels catfish like Kuno normally feed on other fish, frogs, crabs, ducks and rats. The catfish weighed 35 kilos (77 pounds) and had evaded repeated attempts by local anglers to capture him.

Since the dog incident Kuno had become something of a local celebrity. As news of its death began to spread, calls began flooding in from around the world. "The fish has become a mascot for Moenchengladbach," said a city spokesperson.

There was general speculation as to what caused the creature's death. "It could be he died of lead poisoning from the fishermen's weights," observed park keeper Detlef Berschens, "but most of the experts seem to think he just died from old age." Experts, however, believe that low water levels and a summer heat wave probably killed the catfish. There are plans to have Kuno stuffed and mounted at the local Schloss Rheydt museum. Some local residents were not convinced, however, that the dead catfish is the real Kuno. "That's not the Kuno we know," one resident affirmed.

Catfish Court Bouillon

I ran into this recipe while visiting a local boatbuilder. He had knocked off work early in order to cook up a batch of this delightful stuff for his workers and my timing was perfect. Because of the nature of the contents, this is another one that you should not be bashful about altering. It's almost impossible to make wrong. The only drawback is that court bouillon takes quite a bit of time to prepare. I think you'll find that it is worth the work.

1. Sauté the chopped vegetables in the butter or margarine until tender, then add the other vegetables and sauces.

2. Bring to a low boil, reduce heat and simmer for 2 hours, stirring frequently.

3. Cut the fillets into 1-inch cubes and add to the sauce, reduce heat and gently simmer for 30 minutes without stirring. Serve over rice.

Materials needed:

4 to 6 catfish fillets
(2) 14-ounce cans tomatoes
16-ounce can tomato sauce
1 bell pepper, chopped
1 medium onion, chopped
2 cups sliced okra
1 celery stalk, chopped
3 cloves garlic, chopped
1 tablespoon Worcestershire sauce
1 teaspoon +/- Tabasco sauce
1/2 stick butter or margarine

Hefty Catch

"The catfish is well known through the States by its
family name. The cat of the Mississippi is among their
best articles of fish in the market, if not too large.
They often attain to the weight of a hundred pounds.
A friend of mine once took from four night hooks,
hung in the mouths of Rock River, four catfish, whose
united weight was about three hundred pounds."

The General; or, Twelve Nights in the Hunters' Camp
—William Barrows, 1869

Catfish Chowder

Here's one that will knock the chill off a cold and nasty winter day, plus will stay with you for a while. There is no harm in adding additional canned vegetables since original chowder recipes varied widely, mostly along geographic lines. Take a look at Manhattan clam chowder and the New England version of the same thing. They don't even look alike.

1. Over medium heat, sauté the onion until softened and translucent.

2. Remove with a slotted spoon or spatula and set aside. Increase heat and sear the fillets for about a minute on each side and remove.

3. Put the onion back in and add the diced potatoes, lowering heat to medium/medium low. Stir often and cook until the spuds begin to soften.

4. Add enough water to cover the vegetables, put in spices, cover and simmer until soft.

5. Put in the fillets and simmer for 10 minutes or until the fish breaks apart easily.

6. Pour in the milk and cream, lower the heat and stir.

7. Heat until just shy of boiling, remove and serve. Be careful not to boil the chowder since the milk and cream burn easily.

Materials needed:

4 fillets from fish of 2 to 3 pounds
6 tablespoons olive oil
    (You can use butter or margarine.)
1 onion, finely diced
4 medium-sized potatoes, diced
1 quart milk
1/2 cup cream
1 can (12 ounces) whole kernel corn
1 tablespoon seafood seasoning
    (I use Tony Cachere's but there
    are several good ones.)
1/2 teaspoon celery salt
    or celery seed
Salt & pepper to taste

* This is a meal in itself, needing only crackers and a beverage on the side. If you want to make friends, double the size of the batch and share with neighbors when the weather turns foul.

A Civil War Catfish

"An army officer was crossing the Mississippi in a boat rowed by his soldiers, when"... he saw approaching them what appeared to be a large fish, bobbing up and down upon the surface of the water like a porpoise. He handed his sabre to one of the men, and told him to strike it as it passed. The soldier watched his opportunity and gave the fish a vigorous thrust, but the point glanced as if it had struck a bladder. Resolved not to let the creature escape, the man jumped into the stream, and seizing it by the gills managed, with assistance, to get it into the boat. It proved to be a large cat-fish, which had swallowed a musk-rat. The animal's tail still hung out of its mouth."

Harper's New Monthly Magazine
-- August 1867

Succulent Soup

Here we have something of a hybrid recipe. It began as potato soup in a Montana hunting camp, then traveled south to get tangled up in fish cooking. Unlike the gumbo detailed earlier, this dish has a heavier base and will "stick with you" longer. It is a great lunchtime choice after spending a cold morning outside on the water or in the woods. For that matter, it is mighty welcome when your job keeps you out in the weather longer than you would like.

1. Begin by frying the bacon until crisp. Drain and set aside.

2. Pour the grease from the skillet and melt the butter, adding the onion, celery and potatoes.

3. Cook until the potatoes begin to get soft.

4. In your cooker (I like a large glass one with a lid which fits well), heat the milk slowly and add the flour. You may wish to blend these two items before placing in the cooker, if lumps are a problem.

5. Combine all the ingredients, add salt and pepper to taste and put the lid on the pot. Allow it to simmer for 45 minutes to 1 hour. Overcooking is not a problem; undercooking is.

Materials needed:

Medium-sized skillet
4-quart cooker or pot
1 pound of fillets, cubed
6 strips bacon
1 stick butter
1/2 cup chopped onion
1/4 cup chopped celery
2 cups diced potatoes
2 cups milk
1/4 cup flour
Salt & pepper

Easy Fish Quiche

This may sound goofy, but it is good.

1. Boil the fillets in water with salt and pepper for 3 minutes.

2. In a skillet, sauté the bell pepper, white onion and mushrooms in the butter.

3. When these ingredients begin to soften, crumble the fish on top, add the cheddar cheese and pour on top of the whole affair the eggs which have been well beaten with milk.

4. Add salt and pepper to taste.

5. Reduce the heat to low, put a lid on the skillet and leave it alone for 10 minutes.

Materials needed:

Skillet
1 pound of fillets
Salt & pepper
1/4 cup chopped bell pepper
1/4 cup chopped white onion
1/4 cup sliced mushrooms
2 tablespoons butter
1/4 cup grated mild cheddar cheese
6 eggs
1/2 cup milk

Simple Semi-Chowder Casserole

Back when my children were young, my wife and I often worked long hours and odd shifts to keep body and soul together. That meant that dishes that everyone liked and which could be put together quickly took on a high degree of importance. Here is one that I almost forgot when planning this cookbook. It is so easy that you certainly have little to lose by trying it.

1. Spray the casserole dish with your nonstick vegetable spray and lay the fillets, which have been lightly rubbed with lemon juice, in the bottom.

2. Salt and pepper to taste, then slice, dice or chop the onion and pepper if you decide to use the latter and place them more or less evenly on top.

3. Pour on the mushroom soup and 1/4 cup of water. Cook at 275 degrees for 1 hour.

4. If you have a covered dish, cook for 30 minutes at 325 degrees, remove the cover and cook for 10 minutes more. Either way will work quite nicely.

Materials needed:

Pyrex casserole dish
1 pound of fillets
1 lemon
1 can Campbell's cream of mushroom soup (If you like this, try substituting cream of celery next time.)
1 white onion
1 bell pepper (optional)
Nonstick vegetable spray
Salt & pepper
1/4 cup water

Catfish Creole

Catfish Creole is a delightful dish that you can start early and then forget while handling the more labor-intensive aspects of your cookout. As described here, it will feed five or more guests depending, of course, upon their appetites.

Before starting, remove the grill from your smoker/cooker (mine is a Brinkmann), and make a foil boat large enough to cover it leaving just enough room for the lid to fit.

1. Combine all the ingredients except the fillets in a saucepan and bring to a boil, stirring frequently to prevent scorching.

2. Set aside while you arrange the fillets in the foil boat (spray foil with nonstick vegetable spray first), then cover with your sauce.

3. Once your charcoal has burned down to an even gray color and the heat is even, toss in a handful of hickory chips, put the grill rack with your fillets in place and put the lid on.

4. Leave for 45 minutes or more, removing from the heat when the fish flakes easily.

Materials needed:

Enough catfish fillets from a 1- to
  2-pound fish to fill the foil boat.
  Cut the fillets into portions if
  necessary, but maximize your
  space.
3 sticks butter
1 jar of creamy horseradish or
  1 tablespoon freshly grated root
1 tablespoon hot sauce, Tapito's or
  Tabasco preferred.
2 tablespoons Worcestershire sauce
1 tablespoon Dale's Steak Sauce
1 cup lemon juice
1/2 cup red wine vinegar
1/2 cup tomato sauce
Salt & pepper to taste

Fish cookings (we used to call them simply fish fries) these days include a lot more people than those back when the crowd consisted mostly of family and a neighbor or two. For that reason it pays to have something in the works other than just a cooker filled with oil that has to perform duties that include not only the fish, but potatoes and hush puppies as well.

*
Here's an entrée that is perfect over rice, white or wild, and some garlic bread and a salad will make a complete meal if you want to go that route. This is also a great chance to break the old (white wine with fish) rule. Try a nice, smoky merlot instead.

Almost Gumbo

Lack of time for serious cooking and a family's love for gumbo led to another recipe. It can be done in a hurry, and has the advantage of being able to easily handle family members who are different time schedules. While intended for a full meal, the basic "gumbo sauce" can be refrigerated and used later.

1. In your skillet, sauté the onions, peppers and okra in butter until soft.

2. Add salt, pepper, tomato sauce and water. Use 2 cups of water if cooking with tomato sauce or 1 ¼ cups if using cooked tomatoes.

3. Cover and cook over medium-high heat for 15 minutes.

4. If going for a full meal, add the salted and peppered fillets and cook for 6 to 8 minutes over medium heat. For smaller portions, use just enough of the base to cover the amount of fish being cooked.

Materials needed:

Large skillet with lid
2 pounds of fillets
1/4 cup chopped onion
1/4 cup chopped bell pepper
1 cup sliced okra
2 tablespoons butter
Salt & pepper
1 4-ounce can tomato sauce or
   8 ounces cooked tomatoes

* Yeah, it is kind of thick for gumbo, but the taste is right on the button.

Raining "Cats" and...

"The 'Norfolk Argus' states that a curious phenome-
non attended the hail storm in that city on Tuesday
night. Quantities of catfish, some measuring a foot in
length, fell in different sections of the city, and some
of the fields were literally strewed with them.
Hundreds were picked up in the morning. This, says
the 'Argus,' is no piscatorial fabrication, but a fact
which is attested by hundreds of citizens."

Scientific American, June 4, 1853

Spicy Stew

This is sort of a combination of some of the other recipes in this section of the book, but with a couple of additions. One of the rules in preparing a cookbook is to never use a single recipe when you can squeeze at least two out of the same basic set of ingredients.

1. Sauté the pepper, onion and okra in 3 tablespoons butter, then add everything except the fish and simmer on medium heat for 30 minutes.

2. Add the fillets and cover. Leave it alone for 30 minutes, remove the lid and simmer for 5 minutes and serve.

* This is a dish that begs to be served with or over rice.

Materials needed:

Large skillet with lid
    (preferably cast iron)
2 pounds of fillets
1/2 cup chopped bell pepper
1/2 cup chopped onion
1/2 cup sliced okra
3 tablespoons butter
1 can Campbell's cream of
    mushroom soup
1 can Rotel tomatoes
1 can spicy stewed tomatoes
1/2 teaspoon dry,
    ground cayenne pepper
1/4 cup ketchup
Salt & pepper

Jugging

No form of catfishing is more fun than fishing with jugs. Decades ago, folks called it "blocking" because blocks of wood were used to float the participants' catfishing rigs. Today, empty milk or soda jugs are more likely to be used.

Each jug line is made with a piece of strong fishing line of varying lengths with a hook and weight tied to some kind of float—a gallon plastic jug, block of wood, etc.—painted for visibility. Several jugs are dropped into the current and the fisherman drifts along behind in his boat, drawing in the catfish when one of the jugs is seen to move against the current.

Slow-Cooked Fish & Beans

When I received a West Bend Slow Cooker for Christmas a couple of years ago it figured to be one of those gifts that languishes forgotten in a remote closet. Crock pots have never been high on my list of cooking utensils and I mistakenly lumped the Slow Cooker in the same category. Happily, one trial run with it when preparing a pot of beans put me on the right track.

1. Lightly coat cooking pan with vegetable spray, then place salted and peppered fillets in the bottom.

2. Add all the other ingredients, stirring so that they are well mixed.

3. Turn heat to #4 and cover. Leave for 20 minutes.

4. Reduce heat to #2 for 1 hour. There is really nothing to this one and you can serve it right in the cooking dish.

Materials needed:

Slow Cooker
2 pounds of fillets
1 small white onion, chopped
(1) 12-ounce jar salsa
   or picante sauce
1 can red kidney beans
1 can pinto beans
1 tablespoon chili powder
1 teaspoon dry ground
   cayenne pepper
Nonstick vegetable spray
Salt & pepper

Piscatorial Pie *1

Meat pies are a major food item in many countries, but here in the United States about the only ones that you will find are found in the frozen food section at the grocery store. Few people make their own, and even fewer ever experiment with fish when preparing one. That can be a mistake, so I am including two of my favorites for you to try.

1. Place the 2 quarts of water into a cooking pot, add 3 tablespoons of salt and 1 tablespoon of pepper and bring to a boil.

2. Add the fish and cook for 3 minutes. Remove the fish, drain and set aside.

3. Mix the cracker crumbs with 1/3 stick melted butter, knead well and press into the pie pan. Set aside.

4. Sauté the chopped onions in 2 tablespoons of butter in the skillet until barely soft, then add the chicken stock and allow to simmer.

5. Pour the onion mixture into the pie crust and add the catfish, crumbling it as you go.

6. Mix the eggs, milk, salt, pepper and spices and pour over the catfish.

7. Bake at 350 degrees for about 30 minutes or until a toothpick inserted into the thickest part comes out clean.

Materials needed:

8-inch pie pan
4-quart cooker or stewer
Medium-sized skillet
1 pound of fillets
2 quarts water
1 stick butter
1 cup crushed snack crackers
   (not saltines)
2 cups chopped Vidalia onions
2 eggs
1/4 cup chicken stock
   (can be made from bouillon)
1/2 cup milk
Oregano
Salt & pepper

*
Because this is a "meal in a dish" recipe, once again you should feel free to experiment, especially by adding drained, cooked vegetables to the basic ingredients.

Pie *2

This is the more traditional meat pie. You have probably had something similar containing beef, pork or chicken so it will not seem totally alien to you.

1. Prepare the water with salt and pepper as told in the previous recipe and allow the fillets to boil for 3 minutes. Set aside.

2. Sauté the onion in 3 tablespoons of butter until soft, then add the chicken broth.

3. Mix the milk, eggs and vegetables.

4. Divide the cooked fillets between 2 or 3 pie shells and spoon the mixture over the fish. Salt and pepper to taste.

5. Add a top crust, crimping the edges well with a knife and picking several vent holes so steam can escape.

6. Bake at 325 to 350 degrees until the crust is golden brown. Once again, allow to cool before serving. Meat pies hold heat for a surprisingly long time and can singe the unwary.

7. If your pie does not quite have the internal consistency that you like, add 1/2 teaspoon of cornstarch the next time around.

Materials needed:

2 or 3 eight-inch pie crusts, commercial or homemade
4-quart cooker
Medium-sized skillet
1 pound of fillets
1 cup chopped white onion
(1) 12-ounce can whole kernel corn, drained
(1) 12-ounce can carrots & English peas, drained
3 eggs, beaten
1/2 cup milk
1/2 cup chicken broth or bouillon
Salt & pepper
2 quarts water

* Feel free to experiment by adding other ingredients to the pie filling.

Some Final Thoughts

There are many more recipes which do justice to fish, enough for another book to come along later after I have had time to recover from the burns, cuts and smoke inhalation caused by this one. We barely touched smoking on this one, and did not address the use of microwave cooking, a method so dear to our current "hurry up and be lazy" existence. Look for that next time.

Also, bear in mind that there are no absolutes when it comes to cooking. Experimentation is a wonderful thing and I encourage you to do just that with any (or every) recipe herein. The world can never have enough really good food.

–Stan Warren
Bethel Springs, Tennessee, 2003

Acknowledgments

The author would like to express his thanks to those whose assistance made this book a reality.

*My stepfather and maternal grandfather who showed me that fishing was more of a passion than a pastime.

*Those fishing partners who made the past half-century so memorable.

*Pat, my wife who has so often been the guinea pig for some of my more off-beat creations.

*Lodge Cookware for producing and providing their truly excellent cast iron cooking implements.

*The Brinkmann Corporation for the use of their smoker/cookers and charcoal.

Index